MODEL MAKING

MODEL MAKING

HERBERT LOZIER

CHILTON BOOK COMPANY PHILADELPHIA NEW YORK LONDON

Foreword

This book is intended to assist the person who would like to enjoy the pleasures of putting his creative skills to work in the construction of models, working from the simple to the more difficult ones.

It will also serve the more advanced modeler who will find in its pages many things of interest. The serious model collector will discover ways to help him enhance his collection.

The models chosen for construction are mostly those of older planes and cars. The reason for this is that they are easy to construct, and have fewer gadgets or parts to break, or to confuse the new builder.

A most helpful feature of this book is a complete set of working plans drawn to scale which can be followed to construct the model of a soaring glider, a plane, a locomotive, a truck, a racing car, a stunt glider and a boat.

When it is desired to make full size tracings of a plan, it will first be necessary to double the size of the plan by photographic enlarging.

HERBERT LOZIER

Bethpage, Long Island, New York

Contents

MODEL MAKING

Chapter 1

A Short History of Model Making

Models are not always small in size—size has nothing to do with it, for they can be 10 inches long or 10 feet long! Models are either a prototype (the first one of a kind) or a copy of something. To one just starting out, as well as to those who have been building models for a while, the making of models may seem to be something new, or, at the very least, that began not too many years ago. The opposite is true.

Model making is even older than civilized man, for when the caves of pre-civilized man were found, these ancient dwellings contained crude dolls, which are, after all, models of people, and toy animals, which are models of animals. Each of these toys, or models, was made by someone thousands of years before the first great civilization came into existence.

Of all the very ancient peoples, the Egyptians, many of whom were great architects, scholars and astronomers, were outstanding model makers. In the tombs of their kings were found beautiful models, some of pure gold. We call these models statues. But also found were other models besides the statues, which come nearer to representing the things we have today—models of chariots and of ships, each made by a master craftsman and complete in every detail. These

1

Not all automotive model making is done full size. Work is being done here on the front end of a 1937 General Motors car model. This narrow-styled radiator was used on many makes of car. (*General Motors*)

are so perfect that even a copy of one would look beautiful on your shelf.

A little later in history, the Greeks took up where the Egyptians left off. Their great buildings, carvings, sculpture and designs are still looked upon today as guides to beauty and structure. The Greeks made models, too—models of ships, of buildings, of horses and of dolls dressed in the costumes of that ancient day.

After the Greeks came the thousand-year-long civilization of the Romans. They were builders of fabulous monuments, buildings and roads, some of which exist to this day. In a society such as theirs was, it is natural to expect to find models of many kinds, among them ship models. These were models of great galleys, with bows that carried long pointed rams, hulls with many tiers or bands of oars, and a huge, single sail. Many models were made of these galleys or warships of that long-past day and also of the chariots of the Roman army, perhaps as models or prototypes of the real thing.

Models were used by the generals of the Roman army to plan the battles that made them masters of the then known world. We can imagine what these models were—horses, foot soldiers, soldiers on horseback, chariots and battle equipment. Today, the same kinds of models are used, but not always for actual warfare. We are all familiar with toy soldiers—the model soldiers cast in lead and other materials that are so popular with children.

The Phoenicians and the Arabs, too, were great sailors who doubtless made models of the ships they sailed in.

Before making a full-sized clay model, a wooden framework called an armature must be built and properly located to hold the clay. The entire process takes from 800 to 900 man-hours. (*Ford Motor Co.*)

A model maker working on a clay mock-up of a full-sized Corvette.
(*General Motors*)

As time went by, interest in model making was connected with the building of horse-drawn carriages. Wagons of the day took two forms, one to carry freight and one to carry people. The latter type gradually developed into the coach, which was used for public transportation. Although the coach had its beginning in the Middle Ages, it was not until the late 1600s and on into the 1790s that the passenger coach really came into its own. From then on, right up to the time of the invention of the practicable automobile by Daimler and Benz during the 1880s, horse-drawn coaches offered the usual method of transportation, and as such were the reason for making models of them.

The men who built these coaches, called carriage makers, employed not only wonderful designers who turned out many elegant creations, but also model makers who built models of coaches, open carriages and freight wagons for their customers to see before work was begun on the actual vehicle. You can be sure that many a young

The only way to evaluate a styling concept is to see it in three dimensions and in full scale. Completed clay models are painted and trimmed to simulate a steel-bodied car. (*Ford Motor Co.*)

boy living then built models of these just as we make models of the cars we like today.

While all this was going on, ships sailed the oceans, and, with greater distances to cover than ever before, grew progressively larger and faster. Designs gradually changed from the high, tubby ships of the time of Columbus to the swift sailing ships called packets. From packets developed the clippers, the fastest sailing vessels ever built, and also the most beautiful. It is said that Donald McKay, one of the greatest designers and builders of wooden clipper ships in the world, in the early 1800s actually studied the form of dolphins, and then made models of them and applied their shape to ship models until he obtained the hull lines he wanted. He then laid out the plans for his clipper ships. More than one record-breaker came from McKay's New England shipyards, among them the famous "Flying Cloud," "Sovereign of the Seas," "Stag Hound" and "Lightning." All of these can be found today in wood or plastic model kits.

5

Other things were happening in the early nineteenth century, the most important of which, from our point of view, being the development of the railroad. Development of the steam engine began in Great Britain. It is credited to James Watt, who lived from 1736 to 1819. The locomotive, its direct descendant, resulted from the combined ideas of many great inventors. But it remained for George Stephenson, who lived from 1781 to 1848, to make it a practical reality. He is generally given credit for the invention of the steam locomotive.

It is certain that none of these men just went ahead and spent time and money on the real thing right away. Models were built beforehand, and then corrections were made on the model until it was perfected to the inventor's satisfaction. Only then were the working machines built. Many kits are available now for the early locomotives in HO and O gauge sizes.

With the steam engine a proven source of power, it was not long before Robert Fulton and others set a steam engine into a ship, provided it with paddle wheels, and proved that the sail was no longer the ruler of the seas. What Fulton's "Clermont" proved on the Hudson River, the "Great Western" proved on the Atlantic ocean. Before these steamships were constructed, models were made.

Body contours are checked with wooden templates to ensure accuracy. This mock-up is made of clay. (*Ford Motor Co.*)

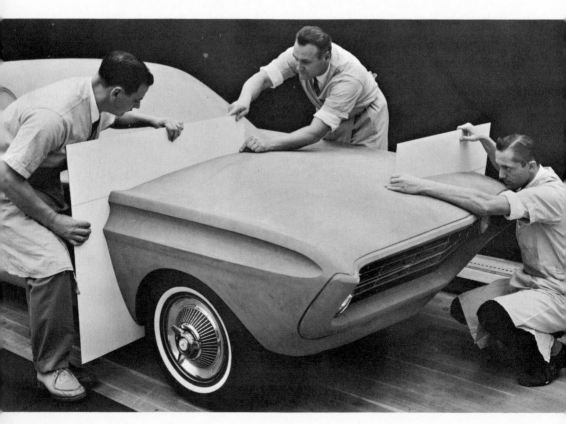

Clay models are often sculptured during the styling of an automobile, and when complete look amazingly real. (*Ford Motor Co.*)

All of the world's great navies use ship models to test design and construction of everything from hulls alone to the detailed, completed ship. Hardly any shipyard in the world—particularly one building large vessels—ever does much work without models as guides.

Many museums show collections of ship models. These often present the complete history of ships from the primitive canoe to the modern ocean liner. It is not unlikely that your local museum has at least one collection and if you ever visit the Smithsonian Institution in Washington, D.C., you can see one of the best model ship collections in the world.

To build a model ship yourself, all you need do is visit your model shop or hobby store and select a ship model in some kind of kit—wood, or plastic, or cardboard—to suit your pocketbook and fit your skill. There is a tremendous variety of sizes, scales and types to choose from.

The serious acceptance of the model in automobile manufacturing came along in the early 1900s when style became as important a part of the motor car as its engine or its chassis. By the time of the First World War, some of the large automobile makers had established

Except for the interior, this mock-up of a full-sized GT Ford racing car in clay is completely detailed. (*Ford Motor Co.*)

their own design and model shops as a permanent part of their manu-facturing facilities, along with their sales and advertising departments. By the 1930s, the making of all sorts of car models in the maker's de-sign departments was an accepted fact. The materials used were wood, clay, plaster and metal.

The general idea is to build a model of clay in small scale to the original design of the stylist. Further work is done on the model until it comes fairly close to acceptance by those concerned with the car, planned, perhaps, for next year's production. Sometimes a larger scale plaster model is made, painted and finished complete with all bright work. This is inspected and changes made once again. New drawings are worked on and now a full-sized clay model or "mock-up" is built. In this way, the designers and the production men begin to see what they actually have.

What once was only a model car on a workbench, or a finished plaster model under a glass case, has now become a full-sized study. Imperfections that did not show up before, such as a poor line here, a curve there, the need to move the bumpers higher or to place the headlight slightly inward, the slant of the windshield, the width of the doors—all faults become visible and are corrected on this full-sized clay model.

But that is not the end of it. Once the clay mock-up has been corrected and finished to suit designers and production men, work is begun on a full-sized model of wood. This wooden car is completely

This full-sized model, called the "V.I.P.," is intended to provide ideas for future styling of production cars. (*Chrysler Motor Corp.*)

finished, inside and out, painted and trimmed. All the grill work, bumpers, instruments, hub caps and ornaments are installed. If you did not know that the car was a full-sized wooden model, you would claim that it was an actual car, made of metal, right off the production line. This car is now as exact as the final manufactured product will be. All the designers, the production men and the men of the sales department give it a final inspection. Everyone now knows what the new car will look like.

There is still another step, because from these full-sized wooden car models are taken the sizes and shapes of the various parts and these patterns are used to make the tools and dies that will soon press, cut and stamp out the many parts of the production cars. It is easy to understand how important model making is in one of the greatest industries in the world.

Kits are available for building model cars that go back as far as the 1898 Peugeot coupé, the Gobron-Brille of 1899, the Renault of 1900. These, however, are of French manufacture and the possibilities are not too good that you will find them in the United States; but models of the 1903–4 Curved Dash Oldsmobile, the Stanley Steamer, the Stutz Bearcat, the Mercer Runabout, the Buick Roadster and others of the early American cars can be purchased.

For a later period you can choose from the great classics of the 1930s. These cars include the metal models made by Hubley, such as the Duesenberg Open Sport Touring and the chauffeur-driven

9

Research is being made into the application of radical missile shapes to automobiles. This is a ⅝ scale model called the "Maxima." (*Ford Motor Co.*)

Town Car. The Packard Touring Car, Roadster and Victoria Coupé can also be purchased. Hubley also builds many other kits.

In plastic there are beautiful classics built by Jo-Han including the Cadillac V-16 Touring and Convertible Coupé and the Mercedes 500 Roadster. Monogram does a wonderful job with cars like the Duesenberg Torpedo Touring Car, the Mercedes 540K Convertible Coupé, the beautiful Rolls-Royce Roadster, the 812 Cord and the Bugatti type 35B.

Of the modern car models there seems to be no end in the selection of plastic kits. The most modern of the modern cars is the Jo-Han Chrysler Turbo Car, which is built like most of these plastic models in the $\frac{1}{24}$–$\frac{1}{25}$ scale size.

Monogram offers two of the finest model kits available in large scale: the English XKE Jaguar and the American Chevy Corvette. Both are built $\frac{1}{8}$ the size of the actual car. Cars built from these two fantastic kits look almost as real as the life-size automobiles.

Then, at the other end of the scale, are the $\frac{1}{32}$ scale models of classics and other cars, besides models of cars that are projections into the future and carry the names of great makes of the past, contained in the easy-to-construct kits made by Renwall. These modern versions of classic cars are the Bugatti 101, the Mercer, the Packard, the Duesenberg, the Stutz, the Pierce-Arrow and the Jordan Playboy. The Renwall cars are kits on which a builder can use his imagination. He can go a step farther than the kit for super detail without the necessity of changing many parts.

The variety of car models available is bewildering; everything is offered from trucks to hot rods and from old to new for a few cents up

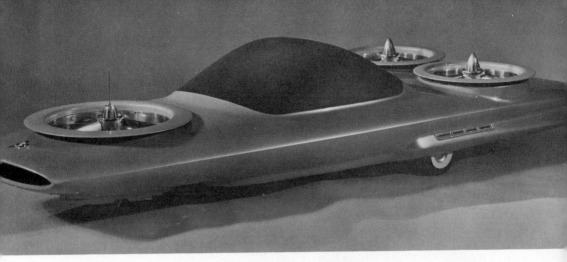

A ⅜ scale model of an aero-car, the "Volante," represents an advanced styling concept of a vehicle that might be able to operate in the air or on the ground. (*Ford Motor Co.*)

to quite a few dollars. Much the same is true with planes.

Even before the Wright brothers made their first flight at Kitty Hawk, North Carolina, in 1903, men were experimenting with gliders and powered models. Someone has said that the early flying machines were nothing more than full-sized flying models with an engine powerful enough to take the airplane and its passengers into the air. One look at the early planes is enough to prove the truth of this statement.

Before men found themselves carried into the air by gliders or powered machines, they constructed models of the flying craft they expected to build later on. Most of the models were more successful than the full-sized finished product, for they flew and the full-sized airplanes did not! A classic example is the powered models of Dr. Samuel Langley, which were successful, although the finished planes never left the ground.

Models were made of gliders, even before the Langley powered models, by the German, Liliendahl, and also by Octave Chanute, of Chicago, who later went on to construct successful full-sized gliders.

As we know, the Wright Brothers are usually given credit for developing the powered aircraft; but long before their first flight they made models of gliders, some of which they flew from the ends of lines like kites. With these large glider models, they experimented with the method of warping wings in order to obtain lateral stability. Today, this action is controlled by the ailerons. The Wrights also built a wind tunnel and in it tested models of wing surfaces and studied wing lift and construction, which they applied to the 1903 Wright flyer. In fact,

11

The "Seattle-ite XXI," a unique six-wheeler with tandem-mounted front-drive wheels, is a ⅜ scale model. (*Ford Motor Co.*)

it can be said that it was models that pointed the way to powered flight.

Other successful early airplanes were the Curtiss biplane, the Bleriot monoplane, the Antoinette, the Avro triplane, the Nieuport monoplane, the Voisin, the Taube monoplane and the Deperdussin, to mention only a few. Some of the above can be modeled from kits manufactured by the Renwall Company. As with boats and automobiles, it is possible to go into your model shop and take your pick of airplane kits in plastic or wood. Models of everything from the Wright Flyer of 1903 right up to the most modern jet transport or fighter can be found. You will find history in model form on the shelves of your hobby stores!

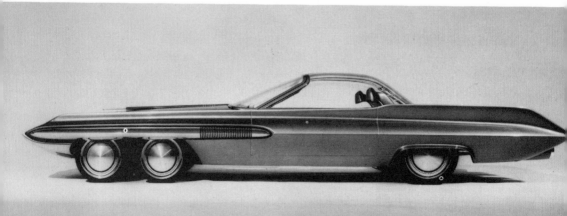

Chapter 2

Tools and Materials

Tools become part of your hands—they do the things that your fingers cannot. A tool should always be used for the purpose it was designed for. You should never use a wire cutter to carve balsa wood or a model knife to shape things out of metal. A round-nosed pliers is not used to bend square shapes any more than a square file is used to make round holes. Always use a tool properly and it will work correctly for you.

Tools should always be kept clean. Glue must be wiped off them and paint removed before it gets hard. Never allow your tools to become rusty. Always keep each tool in one particular place; do not throw them down in a heap. If you do, you will have trouble finding the right tool when it is necessary to pick up a special one for instant use.

Your work table also should always be kept clean and free of leftover bits and pieces. Choose a smooth, flat-top table if you do not have a workbench. If that is not available, it is best to purchase a white pine board about a half-inch thick, cut to the length and width of the space you have to work in. Be certain to choose a board that is not warped. Do not use a piece of hard wood—pine is best because it will take pins and tacks easily and it is not expensive. Pine is always

13

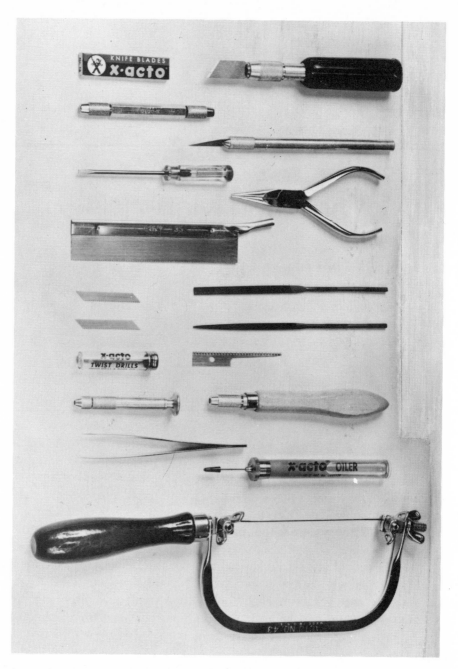

A set of tools like this gives the model maker every advantage and makes finer work possible. (*Kirt Miska*)

available at your local lumber yard. The board you choose can be laid on any table while you work, and removed when work is not being done; or, if you have a permanent place to do your work, the board can be clamped or fastened in place. The working surface should

14

be cleared of any splinters that may get in your hands or in the way of your work.

Wherever you work, on a board placed on a kitchen or card table, or on a workbench in the basement or garage, it is necessary to have good light. You must be able to see what you are building without straining your eyes.

Usually a bulb of 100 watts or more is best. It can be hung over the work place or used in a lamp. In either case, it must be shaded so that it shines down on the table. Arrange it so that shadows do not obscure your work. Sometimes two lights are better than one. It stands to reason that both your working space and the lighting should be correct before you begin to construct your model. Take care of them first.

Now let's think about tools: how they are used and which ones are needed. Some workers will use fewer tools than others. As you work you will discover just how many are needed for you to do your work properly.

For model making, particularly of the kind illustrated in this book, a good cutting knife is the most useful tool. A razor blade of the single-edge type can be used, but it wears out soon and is hard to handle and is dangerous as well. Probably the most available and the best tools made for model making are those manufactured by the X-acto Company of Long Island City, New York. You can purchase them in any hobby shop or in hardware and tool supply stores.

The X-acto knife is most popular with model makers. It comes in many sizes with a great number of interchangeable blades of different shapes. Some of the best ones are the pointed type, used with the slim, light handle. However, you should try several and purchase the one, or ones, you feel will be best suited to your hands and the work you want to do.

In cutting balsa wood, which you will do quite often, the proper knife is a fine friend. If you wish to cut a straight line, the knife should be guided by the edge of a metal ruler, and if you are cutting a curved line, by a metal French curve.

You will, therefore, need metal rulers and French curves. A 12-inch ruler is obtainable in almost any stationery store, hobby shop or hardware store. A French curve may be purchased in a stationery store or in any art supply shop. Like the ruler, it comes in several sizes. If you can afford it, it is a good idea to buy several, ranging from 6 inches to 1 foot in length. You are cautioned not to purchase any not made of metal. A wooden ruler or French curve would soon be cut and made useless by the knife.

Now you have the means of cutting your materials to shape and guides to help you follow your cutting lines correctly. A word of caution is necessary here. Whenever you use knives of any kind, cut *away from yourself* and especially *away from your fingers!* Place your work so that this is always the rule. Never try to cut out a piece in one great slice. Go easy. Take many, not too deep, cuts until your piece is finally separated from the stock.

Of next importance to the knives is the saw. At least three kinds are helpful to have on hand. First get a razor saw. Perhaps the best to use for small model making and balsa-wood work is one that is three-quarters of an inch wide, with fine teeth and a handle that affords a good grip. This tool is excellent for cutting straight edges that must be square, or for making long, even cuts when you find it is easier than cutting with a knife. X-acto makes an excellent razor saw.

The next is a jig saw. Jig saws come in two sections or parts, the handle and the blade. With this saw it is possible to cut shapes that would be difficult, or almost impossible, to cut with a knife—and not split the wood. It is especially useful for cutting curved sections out of thick balsa or pine wood. Here, too, several types of handles and blades are available to the model maker. Usually fine-toothed blades answer model-making purposes best.

For cutting metal without having it curl up, a metal cutting saw is an excellent tool. You may purchase a separate handle, giving you a third saw to save changing the jig-saw blades, or, if that does not bother you, get from your art store dealer, hobby shop or hardware store the metal jeweler's saw blades only, with fine teeth. Sometimes these are hard to come by, but after a while you will be happy you went to the trouble of finding them, particularly when some small piece has to be cut out of metal or plastic.

Remember when using any saw that it is not a good idea to force the saw. Very gentle pressure is actually all that is needed. Allow the saw to do the work, not your strength. If you force the saw, or try to make it go too fast, you will only succeed in breaking the jig saw or the jeweler's blade, both of which are very brittle, or running the razor saw out of its intended path. Blades used in the jig-saw-type handles must be placed under rather strong tension. Never allow a blade to sag. Make certain that the blade is strongly gripped in the fastenings at the ends of the handle and that the fastenings are fixed tightly. Blades should ping when plucked, if they are properly set. Remember to put the blades into the handle with their teeth facing forward.

The next necessary tool is the pliers. They come in all shapes and sizes. The most useful ones for model making are the round- or snipe-nosed, the square- or flat-nosed, the pointed-nosed and the long-nosed types. The best length pliers for model making are 5 inches to about 6½ inches long. Anything larger is too cumbersome when you are handling small pieces. Always try to use pliers that fit comfortably in your hand. Those having smooth rounded handles are best. They should not stick when opening or closing, and must be kept clean so that they always operate smoothly.

The round- or snipe-nosed pliers is the tool to use for bending circular shapes in wire, whether tough piano wire or the pliable brass, iron or copper wire. Various sized and styled hooks can be made up using the round-nosed pliers, such as the propeller shaft hook on the flying models, and the small loops in the landing gear, through which the wheel axles go.

The square- or flat-nosed pliers serves to make shapes that are used in such items as the rear hooks of the flying models, places where right-angle bends must be made. Since they have an excellent grip, they hold all sorts of bits and pieces.

The pointed-nosed pliers is just the thing for handling small items. Little bends are easily made with this tool, either in wire or in most metal pieces. They are good, also, for poking a small part into a hard-to-get-at place.

Pliers that have extra long noses have the advantage of extra reach, and are better to straighten out bends in wire. They hold metal so that it can be sawed or cut better than most short-nosed types do, for the length of the holding surface is greater. Long-nosed pliers can also assist in making bends in cardboard, and will come in handy many times when you work on the truck model, racing car and locomotive. Sometimes it is necessary to grip two pieces of plastic together, either to cut or to glue. Here, too, you will find the long-nosed pliers a very definite help in your construction problems.

When you need to shape small things that cannot be cut or sawed out, a small file is the answer. These small files are usually called Swiss pattern files or needle files, and are a must for making fine, detailed models. Although they can be purchased separately, they are usually sold in sets consisting of from 6 to 12 different styles. They vary from the flat, triangular, half-round, square, round, oval and angular-edged to combinations of the shapes mentioned, and, of course, the files' surfaces also vary from very fine (for polishing work) to rough (for quick cutting). Holes may be enlarged with the round files. Edges can be made to fit better by making them more accurate with the flat file. Curved shapes can be better contoured with the half-round file, and scored lines can be made deeper with the angular-edged file.

There are many more uses for the files, and as you progress in model making you will discover how handy they actually are. Best of all, they are of purposeful use with the plastic kits. All sorts of excess material can be removed with these little files. Edges that do not

17

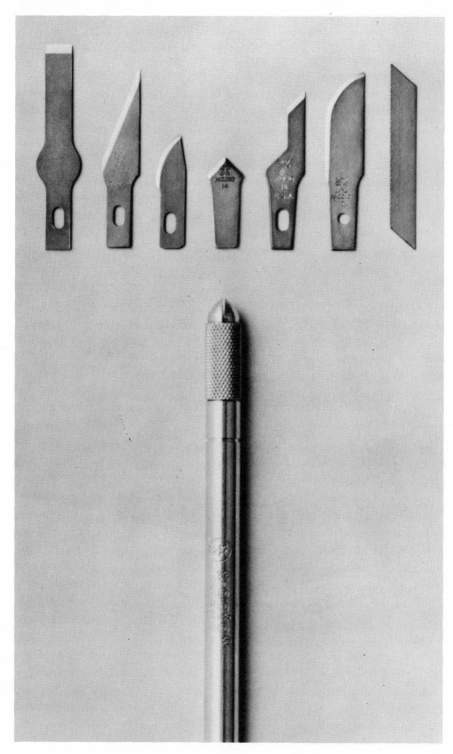

The X-acto knife handle with interchangeable blades helps you do many modeling jobs quickly and precisely. (*Kirt Miska*)

come out of the molds correctly and don't fit properly can be made to do so. Contoured parts can be cleaned up and lines sharpened. Just about the same uses for these files come into play when you are making a kit, or a metal model built from scratch.

An accurate square is also a required tool. If possible, it should have a sliding ruler and a pointed scribe. The best size for model making is one having a 6-inch rule. Don't buy a cheap one. Cheap tools are never good at their best, nor are they the mark of a good workman. It is an old saying that "The work is only as good as the workman, and the workman as good as his tools." You will also find need for a flat metal square, either ruled or plain.

With these tools, edges can be lined up to fit accurately. Horizontal and vertical lines are always brought into absolute alignment and, therefore, are always square to each other. Sections of models like that of the fuselage of the flying model can be checked and it will be noticed immediately if it's in or out of alignment. By placing the square against the sides of the fuselage, the flatness of the uprights and the cross-members against the edges of the square will tell the story. Anything, in fact, that must align perfectly should always be checked out with the square.

The square's ruler will come in handy when it is necessary for you to measure the distance of a fixed crosspiece, and if the part happens to be of metal, the scribe is used to mark it. The scribe can be used also to make guide lines in wood before it is cut or sawed.

Drills are important. Without them you cannot make holes that are true and round. It would be hardly possible, for example, to make the necessary hole in the propeller hanger without one.

A set of drills ranging from number 45 to 80 should give you a good selection. Also, you will need a handle for them (called a pin vise) which is used with the small drills. An electric hand drill or a hand-worked hand drill is necessary for the husky sizes.

Drills come in handy, too, for reaming out the holes in the hubs of plastic, wood or metal wheels, and for drilling through any material where a pin, nail, shaft, or piece of wire must pass. Always remember to fit the size of the drill to the size of the object that is to go into the drilled hole.

If you use an electric hand drill, do not attempt to use it on plastic parts, for it is much too fast and will cause the plastic to melt due to the heat it creates by spinning so rapidly. This jams the drill, and the first thing you know, you have a mess. For plastic material, always use a hand-worked drill revolved at a slow speed. Another thing to remember is never to force any drill. Allow the tool to do the work. Go slowly, for that will prevent improperly drilled holes. It will also help to put the hole exactly where and how you want it.

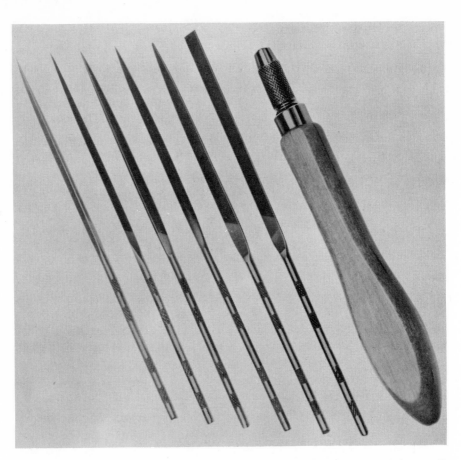

A needle file set for use with metal or plastic models is a handy tool for small shapes. (*Kirt Miska*)

Another tool that is handy for the model maker, especially for building model airplanes, is the balsa stripper. This handy little gadget helps you to cut strips out of flat stock easily and accurately. Using one about 4 inches long, a very comfortable size, strips from $\frac{1}{16}$ of an inch to $\frac{3}{8}$ of an inch wide can be made. You may purchase pre-cut strips at your hobby shop, of course, but sometimes they don't have your size, or perhaps it is inconvenient for you to go there. At such times, you will be glad you have one of these handy little balsa-woodworking tools.

There are times when the handling of a part calls for a tool that is not quite as bulky as pliers. The best thing to use in cases like this is a tweezer. These can be had in many shapes, but those with pointed, and with narrow, flat ends, are the two best suited to model work. X-acto offers excellent ones. Picking up small parts and holding them while gluing or soldering them to another part is the special work of

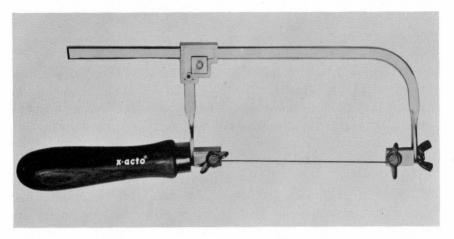

An adjustable jeweler's saw is a necessity when working with brass or other metals and is a great help in cutting plastics. (*Kirt Miska*)

the tweezer in model making. You will find many other uses for them.

Since a considerable amount of wood will be used in building the models in this book, and in most others that you will make later on, the correct sandpaper blocks should be considered important. A great help is the X-acto set of contoured sanders. With these, you can easily smooth off flat surfaces, curved surfaces, pointed ends, narrow slots, rounded parts and V-cuts.

All wood parts will have to be sanded to a smooth finish before they are finished, not only the side surfaces of the part but also the top and bottom surfaces. If you are going to ensure the trueness of all working surfaces, such as the wing ribs of the flying models, sanding will do the correct job. The surfaces of the fuselage and the wings of the glider models, for example, will require careful sanding, as will many parts of the automobile and locomotive models.

Fine paper is always best for a beginner, even though using it may take a little longer. Remember not to press into the work you are sanding, but rather allow the paper itself to smooth the way for you.

A light tap hammer with a magnetized end will help with pins, small nails, or any work that requires deft hammer blows. One with a slim, wooden handle and a head about 3½ inches long is ideal for model work.

Other handy items that come under the title of tools—for they are things to work with that work for us—are such items as cellophane tape, pins, paintbrushes, pencils and waxed paper.

Cellophane tape holds plans down to the work board; it holds parts together while the glue is drying; it mends torn and cut plans and does many other jobs including holding up a part that is painted in order to allow it to dry.

Pins are a necessity, too. These handy little tools work for the model maker by holding the wood parts in place over the plans. They hold cardboard sections together as well, especially since cellophane tape cannot be used to join the cardboard sections of models, for cellophane tape will tear the cardboard surface when you remove it, and that is not exactly what we are looking for. Pins can be made to hold parts together in places where glue cannot be used and where nails are too large and heavy.

Three sizes of pins are good for use with models. About the handiest are the very small ones called lills. These may be a bit hard to find. They come in a box and are usually used for fastening the small labels on wearing apparel. They are not usually used by householders. The medium- and large-sized pins can be purchased in any store that supplies needles and thread, such as the local five-and-ten-cent store.

Using waxed paper is the best way to stop your parts from gluing themselves to your plans or to your work surface. Since it is transparent when placed in direct contact with your plan or drawing, you can readily see through it. Also, the waxed surface will not stick to glue or to the parts of the model. So have a roll handy to place over your plans before you attempt to do any construction that calls for laying your materials directly on the drawings. A piece of waxed paper should be laid between the drawings of the flying models, for example, and the balsa wood that is placed over the plan.

Not too much can be said about glue except to advise you to work carefully with it. Try to keep it off your fingers, a job that is a bit hard to do. Do not use more glue or cement than you actually need. Having the glue spill out of joints is a messy way to work that adds up to a messy model. Except for mistakes with paint, sloppy glue work has spoiled more models than anything else. To apply glue, use a pointed stick. Even a toothpick will do, especially if the glue is the kind that comes in a tube. If the glue is liquid, then a brush usually comes attached to the jar top. Even so, sometimes it is best to use the stick, taking the cement from the brush and then applying it to the parts to be glued. Use a quick-drying glue for wood and cardboard parts, and the special cement that is made for plastic parts. (Plastic cement will not work on wood or cardboard.)

Now we come to the paints. It is the finish that will "make" your model. This is especially true of a scale model. The balsa-wood gliders and flying models in this book need not be painted, but the cars, scale cardboard airplane, locomotive and the boat all call for a paint job.

The question always arises about what paint is best for models. It is suggested that the beginner use the enamel colors found in all

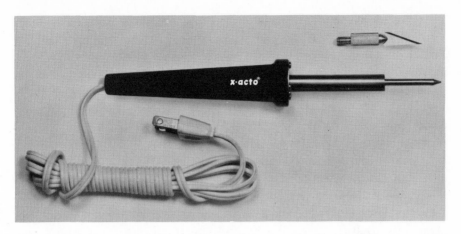

A small soldering iron makes metal working possible. The hot knife is useful in melting plastic parts to form joints. (*Kirt Miska*)

hobby shops and model stores. There is a wide variety of colors, and with some care and a good brush they will give you a smooth, glowing surface. Remember that it is best to flow these paints on rather than to try to brush them on.

When a part is painted, place it in a box with a cover that fits tightly, so that dirt cannot get on the painted surface while it dries. It is best to go slowly and build up the coats rather than to attempt to cover everything at once. The wise thing to do is to thin the paint down a little with a thinner, also purchased where you get your paint, so that when the coats are built up they will not hide details under a blanket of thick color.

As a beginning modeler, you should use a brush to apply paint, although it must be admitted that the spray can is a very easy thing to use when you know how! Use a good, soft brush—one with hairs that will not come out. These cannot usually be found at the five-and-ten, and sometimes not in the model shop. The place to look is the nearest art supply store. At least four brushes should be on hand: a small one with a pointed end for lines and fine work, one with a round end, one with a flat end about ¼ inch wide, and one broad, flat brush about ½ inch wide. Keep the brushes clean when not in use. Thinner will do the job of cleaning. The small pointed-end brush gets into corners best, and the round one puts paint on, generally. The broad, flat brush is best for larger, flat surfaces.

Spray cans should only be used after the modeler has had considerable practice with paint, although a few hints might be given here. First of all, do not hold the spray too close to your work. There should be at least 6 inches between the nozzle and the surface to be sprayed. Always keep the can moving back and forth. Build up

23

the color slowly and carefully by putting on many thin coats until a smooth, shining surface has been reached. Make certain that the part is dust-free before applying any coat. Bits of dust particles may be sand-papered carefully off the surface of either brush coats or spray coats, but one must first make certain that the paint is thoroughly dry. It is good practice to apply paint on an odd piece of wood, cardboard or plastic with either spray or brush before you attempt to paint your model. Get the hang of it first.

The most popular materials for model making are balsa wood, brass, aluminum, cardboard, piano wire and, of course, plastic.

Each of these has its particular use, but it is not unusual to find a kit that includes them all. This is true of the larger gas model airplane kits. Balsa is used for the framework, brass for washers and bushings. Aluminum is used for motor mounts in the gas jobs and for wheel centers, battery boxes and small fittings.

Cardboard finds its place sometimes for cockpit cowlings, nose cowlings, bulkhead stiffeners, dashboards and so on. Piano wire is used for propeller shafts, wing clips, landing gear, rear hooks, tail skids, braces and many other items. Plastic—clear and in color—has become popular for radiators, wheels, propellers, figures, cowl and wheel streamline covers, cabin windows, machine guns, bombs, and radial and V-type engines.

With scratch-built models the builder will use the kind of material that best suits him and the object he is inclined to work on. It is never the same with two model makers—each one has his own likes, naturally. But it is a good idea to follow the rule that the most workable material having the greatest strength is best. This is true mostly when weight is not a factor to be considered.

Usually the scale, non-working automobile models are built of brass sheet. Incorporated in their construction one will find leather for upholstery, wood for interior trim, floorboards, running boards and wheel-spokes. Sometimes, when the real car had it, fabric is used for upholstery as well as for folding tops on the touring cars, roadsters and convertibles. A heavy pile fabric comes in handy for floor rugs inside the car and in the trunk compartment.

Aluminum can be used for dashboards, engine parts (scale non-working engines), side plates, valve covers, oil sumps, engine heads, and—because many engines were all aluminum in the real car— for the engine block itself. The engine can be filed, machined, or sawed out of a single block of soft aluminum, or it can be built up of flat sheet. These are some ways of using this versatile material. Aluminum can be glued together successfully with the clear quick-drying glue and it will, as mentioned, saw, cut and bend to almost any desired shape.

Plastic has already found its way into scale model kits. Indeed, there are so many wonderful kits on the market that it is necessary only to mention that they exist. Ships, airplanes, locomotives and automobiles are available in wide variety.

Probably, though, the least expensive material and the most common is cardboard. It comes with shirts from the laundry and is excellent for model making. Another kind is called "railroad board," and still another is oaktag, the folder material used in office filing systems. The latter is rather thin and pliable but it has many uses, as you will learn once you get into cardboard work. The railroad board costs about thirty cents for a sheet about 3 feet long and 20 inches wide. It comes in many colors but white is best, for you have to paint the model anyway.

Before saying anything more on the subject of cardboard, there is one hard-and-fast rule that you must never forget. Always bend and shape the cardboard *in the direction of the grain.* No matter how small or how large the piece is, remember, *work with the grain.* If you do not, the cardboard will crack, fold unevenly, tear apart, and look dreadful.

Several of the plans in this book call for the use of cardboard almost entirely, yet the models look as good as or better than many others. Working with this material will be a pleasant, new experience for those who have never tried it. The new model maker will find it a delight because of its easy working properties and because it does not crack and break like wood or plastic. It glues together quickly, takes paint well, and makes a light, strong, tough, long-lasting model. It has bending and working properties similar to those of metal. The difference is that it is glued together instead of soldered. However, unlike metal, it cannot be hammered to shape, so several pieces with simple shapes have to be substituted for a formed metal piece. Cardboard is such an excellent material to use for modeling that the firm of F. S. Schreiber of West Germany makes kits using it for everything from aircraft to automobiles, and from ships to castles, all beautifully printed, in full color, and all to scale. Some of these cardboard cut-out models have more details than most of the expensive plastic or wooden model kits have. The super-detailed cardboard models made by Schreiber must be seen to be believed—they are so beautiful.

Painting cardboard requires the same care as for metal or plastic, but no special rules are needed. Any good enamel will do a fine job if you work with care. Use either spray can or brush—it makes no difference to the cardboard.

Cardboard can be made waterproof as well. Preparing a model for waterproofing if, for example, you construct the boat model, becomes a simple job. This is described in the chapter dealing with the cardboard boat. You may also want to waterproof other models you make.

Wood, of course, is the oldest and the best known of modeling materials. It is used to build airplanes, flying or otherwise, and working models of ships as well as scale shelf models. Some of the early model kits for making automobiles were based on wood blocks. They were carved out and boasted such details as windows, door outlines, wheel spokes, tires, lights and bumpers painted on. Locomotive kits, too, were of all-wood construction and one company put out an entire series of historic models. They were of pine wood and most of the details were omitted, leaving it up to the builder to put them on the model.

When wooden models are mentioned, it is the ship model that first comes to mind. Some fantastic kits are available to the ship modeler, running in cost from about fifty cents up to hundreds of dollars. The more expensive ship kits for wood construction have pre-carved hulls and many of the deck and cabin parts are also made up. Some have solid hulls, others are hollowed out, while still others are made up in the same way as the real ships, with planking fixed in place over formed bulkheads. This last method is by far the best, but it is also very difficult for all but the most experienced of builders to tackle.

Usually pine is the wood used for ship models, but white wood, balsa and bass are also used. These are all rather easy to work, and, in the case of the bass and the balsa, they double for aircraft material. Mahogany is sometimes used for the hulls of ship models that are planked or built up, and also for superstructure work. It is used, too, for items in automobile models such as dash boards, interior paneling in closed cars, inside door trim in touring cars and roadsters, and for running boards and various other outside details.

Bass or pine wood is adaptable for the frames of car chassis, and for chassis parts such as springs and axles. Engines may be carved out of these woods as well. In the case of the old racing car described in this book, pinewood was used for the motor hood and the floor boards.

Since the flying models, gliders and rubber-powered airplanes are also made of wood, mention must be made of them. Here, very light, strong balsa wood is employed, and except for the paper, wire and rubber, it makes the entire model. The gliders, in particular, are all balsa. Nothing else is used for the wings and the fuselage. Balsawood may be used as well for small parts of scale models that must be carved out, when either time or availability makes it necessary to substitute it for the sturdier and heavier woods.

In addition to all the materials already mentioned, various odds and ends can be used successfully in model work. Such unlikely things as paper clips sometimes provide just the thickness of wire you may need for a variety of parts. Even the U-shaped ends come in handy and are actually pre-formed for you!

Certain sizes of leathercraft snap fasteners can be used for automobile wheel hubs, and rubber O-rings that you find at your hardware dealer's make excellent tires for scale model cars. Even the aluminum foil that is used in the kitchen comes in handy for such items as running board trimmings, front floor boards, fire-wall facings and dashboards on the automobile models.

The adherent plastic sheets that have a wood grain and are sold for kitchen trim uses are wonderful, especially in mahogany grain, for use on almost anything that you want to make look like real wood. Actually, the boat model to be built from plans in this book could have its upper hull covered with this self-adhering material and in no time you would have a mahogany planked hull! This material can be found in hardware and 5-and-10-cent stores.

The very small nuts sometimes used in radio sets and for model locomotives, HO scale, make excellent hub cap fittings for the older type model cars. Fill in the round threaded opening with model putty, cement them in place, and you'll see how real they appear!

Even the fine screening that is used for tea strainers makes beautiful automotive radiators and side hood ventilation coverings for the antique and classic car models. It can also be used in ship models for gratings, ventilator covers and anything that has a meshwork-like appearance.

Truly, hundreds of common things can be used that are found around your home. Finding and adapting them can be a lot of fun, a work saver, and a surprise.

Many fittings and parts that are sold for models other than the one you may be constructing can be used for your project. Things that are made for ship models can often be used as various automobile components. Things meant for locomotive models can be used for ship models, and parts for cars are adaptable for either ships or locomotives. Take a look about you when you go into your hobby shop. Let your imagination take over. You will see that besides the balsa wood, the bass wood, the brass and aluminum sheets, the paints and the kits there are many other items that will aid you and help to improve your model and your model making.

Chapter 3

An All-Balsa-Wood Stunt Glider

This simple glider is an excellent flying and stunt model. Its construction is so simple that anyone already familiar with airplane model making, or even a beginner, can construct it without effort or mistakes. To be assured of the beautiful flying qualities of this model, it is necessary to follow both plans and instructions closely. Do not try to make up your own changes or to improvise as you go along.

First of all, read this chapter telling you how to make the glider. Next, look at the plans. Study both until you know exactly what you will do before you start construction—where each part goes and how you will put it where it belongs.

Next, look at the list of materials. If you do not have the balsa wood on hand, you will have to purchase it, of course. When you do, make certain that it is wood of the same measurements given in the list of materials. Do not try to glue two pieces together to obtain the correct thickness, for the glue will make the piece too heavy. The piece may also break apart or warp out of shape. Avoid trouble by being exact from the beginning.

The materials you will need to build the stunt glider are:

One piece of balsa wood 11⅛ inches long, ½ inch wide, ⅛ inch thick. (This is for the fuselage.)

One piece of balsa wood $3\frac{3}{8}$ inches long, $1\frac{7}{8}$ inches wide, $\frac{1}{16}$ inch thick. (This is for the fin.)

One piece of balsa wood $7\frac{1}{2}$ inches long, 2 inches wide, $\frac{1}{16}$ inch thick. (This is for the elevator or stabilizer.)

Two pieces of balsa wood $6\frac{1}{4}$ inches long, $2\frac{1}{2}$ inches wide, $\frac{3}{32}$ inch thick. (Or you can use a single piece 13 inches long, cut it in the middle, and use one piece for the right and the other for the left side of the main wing. Do not use balsa wood that is soft or that has stringy black lines running through it. Select clear, hard balsa for all your glider parts.

Now let us assume that you have the materials and the plan ready. The next thing to do is to transfer the plans by tracing them on smooth cardboard, using carbon paper. This will give you working patterns. Trace the profile of the fuselage, then the stabilizer, then the fin, and finally one half of the main wing. Since both sides of the main wing are exactly the same, one pattern will be enough. You simply trace around the pattern twice.

When the parts have been traced on the cardboard (an ordinary laundry-type, shirt cardboard is fine for this), cut out the cardboard pieces. Be careful to do a good job of making the straight lines straight, and curve the fuselage and the wing tips accurately.

Now you have your patterns. Lay these patterns on the correct balsa-wood pieces. Make certain that they fit. It is a good idea to sandpaper the balsa wood lightly before you trace around the patterns in order to get a better and clearer line on the smoothed surface. Try not to press down too hard with a sharp pencil when you go around the edges of the cardboard patterns. It is best to use a soft lead pencil —number 1 or number 2.

When each part has been marked or outlined on its particular piece of balsa wood (fuselage, fin, elevator, main wing), you can start to cut each one out. It is a good idea to do the fuselage first. This is the sturdiest piece; if you are new to modeling, the strength of the $\frac{1}{8}''$-thick balsa will be of some help to you in getting the feel of things.

At first do not cut right to the marked lines. Using an X-acto knife with a pointed blade, carefully keep your cut about $\frac{1}{16}''$ away from the lines. Use a steel ruler to help obtain straight lines, and a metal French curve to help obtain curved lines.

When you have cut away most of the extra wood from the fuselage, wrap some fine sandpaper around your sandpaper block. Very carefully sandpaper away the rest of the wood until you come down to the exact outline of the fuselage. Notice that the top of the fuselage is level and flat. At the bottom and going toward the rear, you will notice that the fuselage has a long straight line. Only the forward part of the fuselage, top and bottom, is curved. An X-acto sanding kit will come in handy here.

29

Balsa-wood stunt glider parts and some of the tools used in making them.
(*Kirt Miska*)

Once the fuselage has been brought down to the exact outline, gently go over the entire fuselage, both sides and top and bottom, with extra fine sandpaper. However, make certain that the top of the fuselage where the wings go is absolutely square to the sides; otherwise, the result will be a lopsided-looking glider.

Next, gently round the edges of the bottom and the front of the fuselage so that when you look at it from the front it will have a U-shaped cross-section. When the sanding has been completed, set the fuselage aside and begin to make the fin.

Since the fin is not a movable surface, it is glued directly to the top of the elevator.

Cut out the fin with care. Trace around the pattern with a pencil. Now cut away the extra wood with your knife and try not to split this thin balsa-wood piece. Sandpaper it down until you are exactly on the outline. Next check and make certain that the trailing edge, or rear, of the fin is absolutely square (at right angles) with the bottom of the fin.

Very carefully, laying one edge of the fin at a time about $\frac{1}{16}''$ beyond the edge of your working board, taper the surfaces a little; one side, then the other, but not the bottom, for this goes against the top of the elevator. Looking at the fin from the top, from the back, or from the front should show you edges tapered to a slight wedge shape. However, do not try to make a knife edge anywhere. Just taper the edges gently to effect a streamline.

The elevator is also made of $\frac{1}{16}''$-thick balsa wood. Sandpaper the wood until it is smooth. Then use your cardboard pattern and

30

trace around it very carefully to make sure that both sides and wing tips are exactly the same.

Use a steel straightedge (ruler) as a guide when you cut the trailing edge and the tapering leading edge. After that, work slowly about the tips until you have come almost to the traced line.

Now, doing exactly as you did to the leading and trailing edges of the fin, use sandpaper to finish and streamline all the edges, as well as the tips. Once again you are reminded not to bring the edges down to a knife edge, but rather to a gently streamlined shape. Never disturb the outline of the elevator. When you have finished this part you are ready to work on the main wing.

You will notice that the main wing of this stunt glider has a sweep-back just as the modern jet planes have. It is because of this sweep-back that it is necessary to make the main wing in two separate sections, one right and one left.

The main wing is heavier balsa than either the stabilizer or the fin to enable you to give it an aerofoil section which will help to create extra lifting power. The general aerofoil shape across the wing is shown on the plans as section A.

Beginning the same way as you did before, sandpaper the balsa wood carefully. Then make a pattern of cardboard. You need make a pattern for only one half of the wing, as mentioned before, since both sides are the same, and so you actually cut two pieces to the same shape. They become the right and the left sides of the wing when they are finished.

Trace around your cardboard pattern onto the two balsa pieces that you have chosen for the main wing. When that is finished, with a steel ruler as guide, cut out the trailing and leading edges of both parts of the main wing. Then work around the wing tips, leaving about $\frac{1}{16}''$ clearance.

Lay the two wing sections on top of each other to see how closely they match. Leading and trailing edges should conform to each other.

When you have sanded away any irregularities, carefully fix the wing sections together, sandwich-like, with cellophane tape. They should not move in any direction. Do not fasten them so tightly that the wood splinters (or worse, breaks) when you remove the tape. Also make certain that your marked pencil lines face outward.

Now that the pieces have been fastened together, sandpaper them down to the exact outline. Doing both pieces together will allow you to make both wings exactly the same. Take your time and see to it that the wing halves match both the plan and each other.

Remove the tape very carefully. Then proceed to make the aero-foil section on each wing half. Only the tops of the wing halves are sanded down. Make certain that you make a right and a left aerofoil section, which can be assured by laying the pieces alongside each other in the same manner as they will go when glued together. Sandpaper the leading edge round on each piece. Next taper the rear trailing edge, first on one section and then on the other. Once again be careful that the trailing edges are not knife-edged.

Do not attempt to make one part of the wing at a time conform to the aerofoil section. Work all along the wing from the center to the tip, doing your shaping with the wing halves lying on your flat, smooth work board or bench. You can make some sort of pattern template to assure the same shape of the wing all along the upper surfaces, if you wish.

When the tops of the wings have been sandpapered to the aerofoil shape, turn the wing halves over and round in the bottom of each leading edge. The front of each wing half should then look rounded with the wing cross-shape looking like section A on the plans.

To give the glider greater stability, a very deep dihedral angle is given the main wing. (Dihedral means the upward angle of the wings from a horizontal plane.) The height of the dihedral angle is usually measured at the wing tips. Our model has a 1¾" dihedral.

Both halves of the wing are glued together at the center. In order to obtain the correct upward tilt of each of the wing halves, prop up the outer end of each side with books or wood blocks. It's easy to do. Using a quick-drying glue at all times, put glue on the inner end of each half. Join the two wing halves together, set them over a small strip of waxed paper, and let them dry a little before you insert the blocks, or books, beneath the wing halves. Do not let the glue dry thoroughly or you will have to break the wings apart in order to make the dihedral.

After you have allowed the glue to set a bit, carefully lift up one side and then put a book or block beneath the wing. Slowly push it toward the center until the wing tip is 1¾" above your workbench surface. Then do the same thing to the other side. Make certain that you do not move the side already propped up. Just to make sure, measure both tips and, if necessary, re-adjust the blocks for the 1¾" height above level. Check and make certain that the center of the joined wing is flat on your workbench and that leading and trailing edges of each half are all on the same plane. At 3" out from the center, the bottom of the wing, front and rear, should be exactly ¹⁵⁄₁₆" above your working surface. You can also use the two wedges shown on the plan to assist you in obtaining the correct dihedral.

When the center section is thoroughly dry and the dihedral fixed, lay a ¼" strip of old bedsheet with glue on it over the center section on the top. Make sure that there is enough glue to get the cotton strip to hold well. Allow it to dry. Be careful that you do not disturb the dihedral angle while doing this important reinforcing job.

Now that all the parts are constructed, you are ready to assemble your stunt glider. Before you glue the main wing in place, you can add a thin piano-wire skid to the nose of the fuselage. Simply cut off a length of flexible wire 2½" long. Bend it into a slight bow, as shown on the plan, and insert about ½" into the balsa. Place a drop of glue where the skid enters the fuselage in order to make certain that it will hold.

Next, place the elevator on top of the fuselage and see that it sits evenly and at right angles to the fuselage. If the top of the fuselage is not square, sandpaper it until the elevator has a perfectly level surface on which to rest.

Put glue between the bottom of the elevator and the top rear of the fuselage. Place the elevator in position. If necessary, hold it with small pins until the glue has dried. You can hold the fuselage upright between two books while the parts are drying.

After the elevator is fixed firmly in place, take the fin and add glue to the bottom. Make sure that the sloping leading edge goes to the front. Glue the fin to the exact center top of the elevators. The fin must be absolutely straight, front to rear, and exactly vertical, or the glider will fly in circles.

Either small wood blocks or small pins can be used to hold the fin in place until the glue has completely dried. Keep using the books to hold up the fuselage while the fin is being fixed in position.

When everything at the tail end has dried, check again and make certain that all parts are at right angles to each other.

Now that you have this taken care of, you are ready to glue the main wing in position. This positioning should be carefully checked against the plan. Notice that the leading edge sticks out just about ¹⁄₁₆" beyond the top of the fuselage.

Put a liberal amount of glue on the bottom of the center of the wing and then put it in position exactly as shown on the plan. Use books to prop up the fuselage and then hold the wing in position, either by pushing two small pins through the center line of the fuselage or by placing blocks or books at the wing tips. However you do it, it is necessary to make certain that the main wing, like the tail surfaces, is exactly square with the fuselage.

Looking at the glider from the front, the tail surfaces should appear absolutely square (at right angles) to each other. The fuselage and the main wing should have exactly the same dihedral angle on each side and should also appear to have the same alignment with each side as with the tail surfaces. All flying surfaces must be in a straight line compared to the centerline of the top of the fuselage.

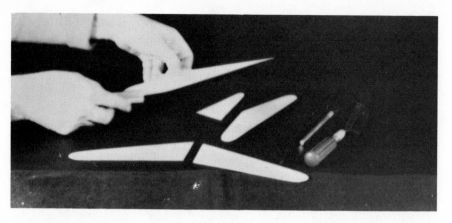

Sanding the nose of the fuselage of a balsa-wood stunt glider. (*Kirt Miska*)

Everything is ready, now that the glue has dried, to give the model a spraying with clear model spray. It comes in a pressure spray can and can be purchased for about 70 cents at any model store.

Hold the spray can about 6 inches away from the model and keep it moving steadily back and forth at an even rate of speed while you press the button on top. A light spray is enough, but cover the entire model. This process will add strength to the balsa and will help to prevent nicking or tearing away of small pieces when rough landings are made. Do not use more than one light spraying or too much weight will be added to the glider and it will not fly well. Allow the spray coat to dry thoroughly. Then, if you wish, you can go over the entire piece with very fine sandpaper, but this is not absolutely necessary.

The glider is now ready to make its first flight. In order to get it to fly, you will have to weigh the nose down. There are several ways to do this. First, you can cut out a hollow, as indicated on the plans by the dotted lines, fill the hollow with modeling clay until the correct weight is obtained, and then cover the clay with cellophane tape. Or you can simply add one or more 1″ 16-gauge brads to each side of the nose of the fuselage and hold them in place with cellophane tape wrapped about the fuselage.

However you choose to do it, you must test the glider first. Do this in a clear spot with high grass if possible. Avoid testing it on the street or any place where there are rocks or automobiles, for when hitting curbs, rocks and autos balsa nicks and breaks very easily.

Take the fuselage between your thumb and forefinger, face the nose slightly downward, and gently throw the glider away from you in a straight line. The glider should fly and flop upward and then fall

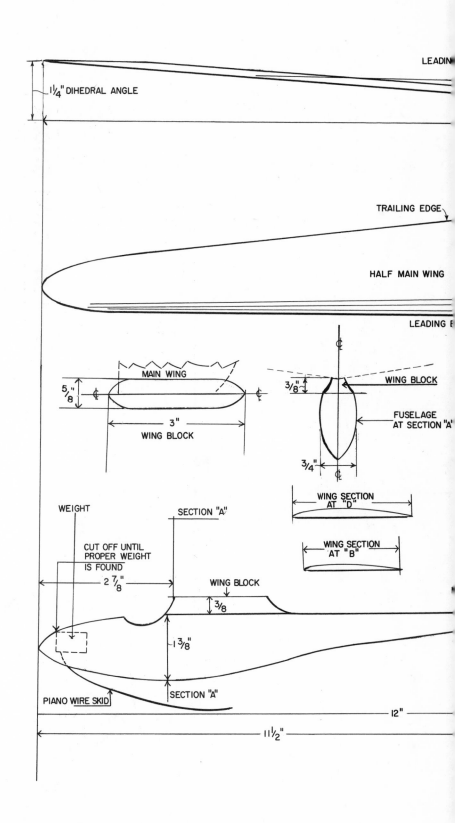

LEADIN

1¼" DIHEDRAL ANGLE

TRAILING EDGE

HALF MAIN WING

LEADING E

MAIN WING

5/8"

3"
WING BLOCK

3/8"

WING BLOCK

FUSELAGE
AT SECTION "A"

3/4"

WING SECTION
AT "D"

WING SECTION
AT "B"

WEIGHT

SECTION "A"

CUT OFF UNTIL
PROPER WEIGHT
IS FOUND

2 7/8"

WING BLOCK

3/8

1 3/8"

PIANO WIRE SKID

SECTION "A"

12"

11½"

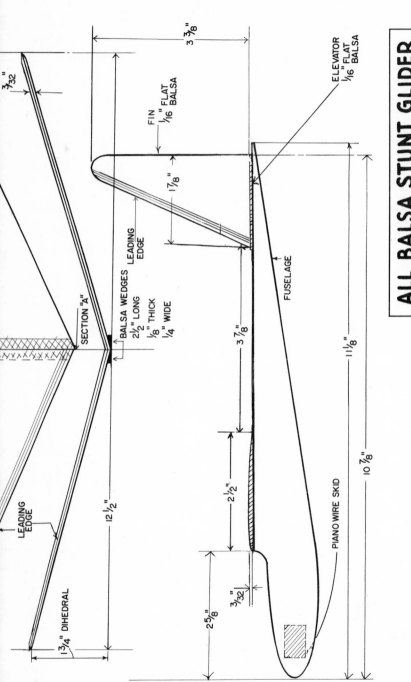

ALL BALSA STUNT GLIDER

$\frac{3}{32}$"

$3\frac{3}{8}$"

FIN
$\frac{1}{16}$" FLAT
BALSA

$1\frac{7}{8}$"

ELEVATOR
$\frac{1}{16}$" FLAT
BALSA

SECTION "A"

BALSA WEDGES
$2\frac{1}{2}$" LONG
$\frac{1}{8}$" THICK
$\frac{1}{4}$" WIDE

LEADING
EDGE

FUSELAGE

$3\frac{7}{8}$"

$11\frac{1}{8}$"

LEADING
EDGE

$12\frac{1}{2}$"

$2\frac{1}{2}$"

PIANO WIRE SKID

$10\frac{7}{8}$"

$1\frac{3}{4}$" DIHEDRAL

$2\frac{5}{8}$"

$\frac{3}{32}$"

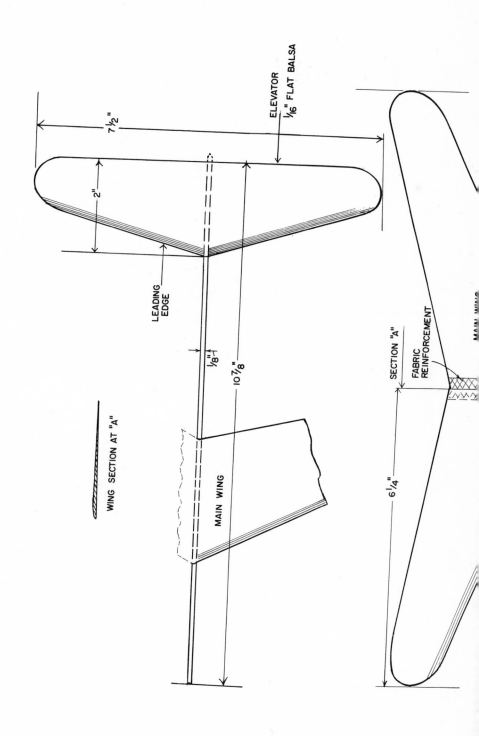

WING SECTION AT "A"

7 1/2 "

2"

LEADING EDGE

ELEVATOR
1/16 " FLAT BALSA

1/8 "

10 7/8 "

MAIN WING

SECTION "A"

FABRIC REINFORCEMENT

MAIN WING

6 1/4 "

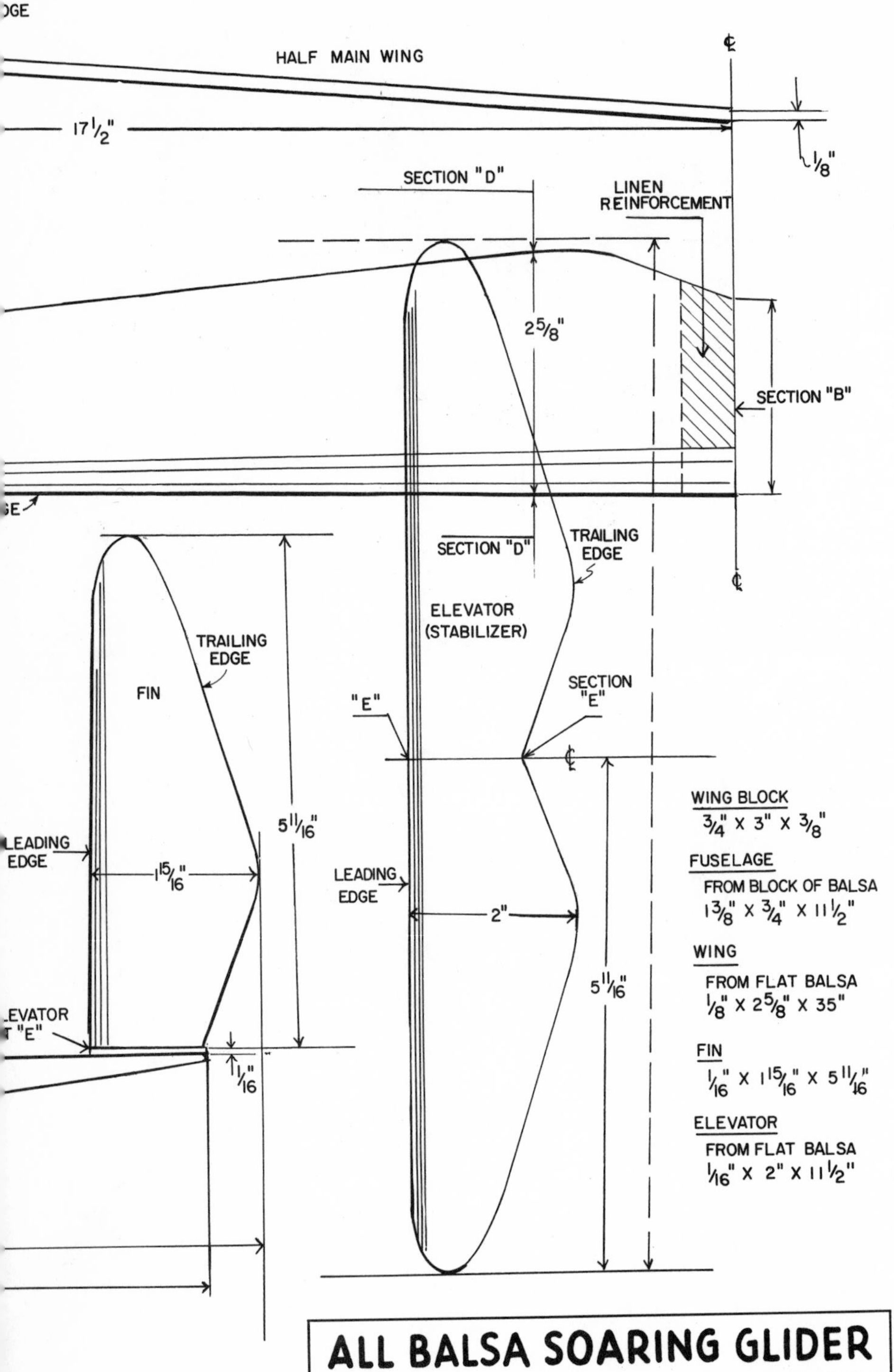

DGE

HALF MAIN WING

¢

17½"

⅛"

SECTION "D"

LINEN
REINFORCEMENT

2⅝"

SECTION "B"

GE

SECTION "D"

TRAILING
EDGE

¢

ELEVATOR
(STABILIZER)

TRAILING
EDGE

FIN

"E"

SECTION
"E"

¢

WING BLOCK
¾" X 3" X ⅜"

5¹¹⁄₁₆"

FUSELAGE
FROM BLOCK OF BALSA
1⅜" X ¾" X 11½"

LEADING
EDGE

1¹⁵⁄₁₆"

LEADING
EDGE

2"

WING
FROM FLAT BALSA
⅛" X 2⅝" X 35"

5¹¹⁄₁₆"

FIN
¹⁄₁₆" X 1¹⁵⁄₁₆" X 5¹¹⁄₁₆"

EVATOR
"E"

1¹⁄₁₆"

ELEVATOR
FROM FLAT BALSA
¹⁄₁₆" X 2" X 11½"

ALL BALSA SOARING GLIDER

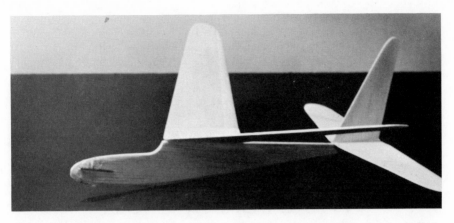

The completed balsa-wood stunt glider with nails taped to the nose for ballast. Many flights were made before this picture was taken. (*Kirt Miska*)

down. Place some clay or two brads (nails) on the fuselage nose and test it again.

If the glider shoots gently downward in a straight, shallow line, you are on the right track. If you have the weight just right, it will glide and dip gently.

Since most models need a bit of coaxing in order to make them fly, it may be necessary to add more weight, but if the glider dives hard, take some of the weight off. If it noses upward and flounders, add a bit more weight. If it still does not fly but gently dips downward, tilt the rear of the elevator slightly upward on both sides. Moisten the wood near the trailing edge with hot water and carefully bend upward. If you do not want to do that, carefully slice the elevator away from the fuselage with an X-acto knife for about three-fourths of the distance forward. Insert one or more $\frac{1}{8}$" by $\frac{1}{16}$" by $\frac{1}{4}$" pieces of balsa near the trailing edge until the glider flies correctly. Hold the elevator to the fuselage with cellophane tape while you insert the balsa-wood bits. Then glue the wing with the balsa inserts solidly to the fuselage once more. Do not forget to keep the tail assembly square to the fuselage.

Properly built and correctly adjusted, this glider will fly very well and many wonderful flights can be made. It will twist and loop and soar and keep your interest, and that of your friends as well, for a long time. Best of all, it will have started you on the happy road to model making and teach you how to handle tools, as well as some principles of aircraft balance and flight. It will make construction of our second glider, a soaring type, an easier task—one that you can look forward to undertaking with enthusiasm and the knowledge that you now have some essential model-making experience.

Chapter 4

The Soaring Glider

Our second project is another all-balsa glider. However, this glider is far different from the stunt aircraft you have constructed. You will notice that the wings are very long, measuring 35 inches from tip to tip. Also, the fuselage is considerably wider and has much more shape to it. There is an aerofoil section to the main wing that is much more pronounced than that of the stunt glider. The fin and the elevator, too, have greater surfaces and are more graceful in shape. Instead of being mounted on the fuselage itself, the main wing is placed on a wing block, thus putting it on a plane different from that of the elevator or stabilizer.

If you look at the drawings, you will realize that now you are beginning to construct a flying model that bears a closer resemblance to the real thing both in form and in flying ability.

The first thing to do is to become acquainted with the plans—to become familiar with the drawings and to know what you are going to do and how you will do it. Visualize how you will make each part and how it will be joined with other parts to create a finished glider. Of course, you should read the complete chapter before starting. With this instruction as guidance, together with your own planning, you will discover that the actual work is greatly simplified and things that appear difficult at first actually are not difficult at all.

First gather your materials. You will need clear, first-quality hard balsa wood for all of the glider parts. For the fuselage, a block of balsa wood 1⅜″ by ¾″ by 11½″ is used. The main wing, made in halves, uses a 3-foot-long, flat plank ⅛″ thick by 2⅝″ wide. You probably will have to buy a piece 3″ wide. The fin and the elevator are made of flat balsa 1/16″ thick. Since both are the same thickness, it is necessary to purchase only one sheet of balsa wood 1/16″ thick, 2″ wide and 18″ long. The wing block or wing mount is made of a piece of scrap balsa wood 3″ long by ¾″ wide by ⅜″ thick. Do not become confused about this block. It is made separately and glued to the top of the fuselage. Do not attempt to make it in unit with the fuselage.

You can work by going according to the measurements. Only one half of the main wing need be drawn, and one half of the stabilizer. Since both sides of these are the same, for the second half all you have to do is reverse your pattern on the wood in order to obtain the entire shape.

First make an accurate cardboard pattern of the fuselage profile. Note that the top of the fuselage is flat looking from the pilot's cockpit to the back, as seen from the side. Because the fuselage is the most difficult part of the glider to shape, make this unit first.

Small pins or cellophane tape can be used to hold the fuselage pattern in place while you trace around it. Trace around your pattern carefully with a pencil on the balsa-wood block reserved for the fuselage. This will give you the shape for the profile or side of the fuselage. Your pattern should be placed on the block in such a way that the straight rear line of the fuselage from the cockpit to the back lines up with the top of the block. Doing it in this way gives you one less surface to carve and sandpaper. Besides, you usually can count on the accuracy of the squareness of the purchased balsa-wood block. If you wish to be sure, you can check the squareness of the fuselage block with a carpenter square. With a jig saw, trim away all the excess wood, leaving about 1/16″ distance between the saw cut line and the penciled line. Do not sand down at one place only, but take off the excess all along the outline. When you have just about reached the pencil outline, start to use finer sandpaper and work right into the marked line.

Assuming now that the profile of the fuselage has been trimmed to shape, your next step is to taper the bottom to a U-shape and to sandpaper the top of the fuselage slightly inward, as shown on the drawing section marked A. This is the cross-section of the fuselage just in back of the cockpit. The front and the rear of the fuselage gradually taper from it, creating a streamlined shape.

Note that the flat top of the fuselage, from the cockpit to the rear, should sand down to about ⅜″ wide because of the slight inward curve given to the upper part of the fuselage following the cross-section shape of A. The nose end is oval-shaped, top and bottom. Also note that the shape of the wing block, shown on the plan and given as ¾″ wide, is made to this measurement first. The block is then glued in place on the fuselage. When the glue has dried, sand down the block to match the sides of the fuselage and narrow the top so that it has a width of approximately ¼″. This shape can be best understood by following the contours indicated by section A. The front of the wing block is matched to the curve of the cockpit by sanding, and then worked down to the top rear of the fuselage by the same method. Be careful when sanding the rear of the wing block that you do not create a hollow in the fuselage where the two meet.

In order to weigh the model down later on, you can cut off the nose of the fuselage as indicated on the plan by the dotted line, and hollow out a cavity to take weight when the glider is ready for its first flight. Or, you may simply want to leave the fuselage alone and weigh it externally. We shall go into that later on.

The tail surfaces are to be made next. These are rather simple. Take care when you make up your patterns of cardboard that you do not confuse the halves of the stabilizer for those of the fin. In order to prevent this, you can make the pattern of the stabilizer as a whole wing instead of as a half wing.

Trace around the fin pattern first on to the ⅟₁₆″-thick balsa. This will give you some feel of the curved outlines of the flying surfaces. If you make a mistake here, it is easy enough to correct it or to make a new fin.

After you have traced the fin and lined up the leading edge of the pattern with the edge of the plank, you can cut out the fin. Either of two methods can be used: you can saw it out or cut it out with an X-acto knife.

Either way calls for caution with respect to accuracy and to keeping your fingers out of the path of the tool. Leave about ⅟₁₆″ between your cut and the pencil line just as you did with the fuselage. Take off the excess balsa wood with fine sandpaper until you are into the pencil line. Take care that you do not split or crack the flat wood. This piece, naturally, will not take the same rough handling as the fuselage block.

When you have the fin outline accurately made, begin to round the leading or front edge. Round it very carefully, using fine sandpaper, right up to the curved tips.

When the leading edge has been rounded, lay the fin on the edge of your workbench and, beginning from approximately ½″ in from the trailing or rear edge of the fin, start to taper down first one side and then the other until an aerofoil or streamlined shape has been obtained. Be careful not to bring the trailing edge to a knife edge, for this would make the trailing edge thin, very weak, and easily broken. Allow slightly more than $\frac{1}{64}$" thickness of the wood along the fin's trailing edges.

Make the stabilizer, or elevator, the same way you made the fin. The outline is traced around a cardboard pattern. Line up the leading edge of the pattern with the edge of the plank. Laundry shirt cardboard should be used for all of the small parts; however, it will be necessary to use showcard for the cardboard pattern of the main wing.

Do not forget to allow at least $\frac{1}{16}$" between the pencil line and your cut. The elevator may also be cut out with an X-acto knife, or you may use a fine-bladed jig saw. Take the excess down with fine sandpaper right to the penciled line. You should also remember to handle this with care, for the $\frac{1}{16}$"-thick balsa wood is easily broken.

After the outline of the elevator is finished, begin to shape its aerofoil, or streamline. Do this in exactly the same way as you did the fins. Round the leading or front edge and taper the trailing or rear edge from about $\frac{1}{2}$" in. You may taper both top and bottom of the trailing edges of the elevator, or just one. In case you decide that only one is necessary, make certain that the tapered trailing edge is on top when you mount the stabilizer to the fuselage later on.

Using a piece of showcard or similar weight cardboard, make a pattern for the main wing. Half of the wing is all you need. It will measure $17\frac{1}{2}$" from tip to center line and be $2\frac{5}{8}$" wide at section D.

Using the $\frac{1}{8}$"-thick balsa-wood plank, trace around the cardboard pattern with pencil. You may use the edge of the wood plank for the leading edge, so line up your cardboard pattern along it. Do this tracing twice. You will have two separate halves after they are cut out, one for the right and one for the left side of the wing. The reason for making the wing in halves is because a dihedral is used. The wing rises $1\frac{1}{4}$" upward from level at the tips.

Allow the usual $\frac{1}{16}$" between your cut-out and the pencil line. Either jig saw or X-acto knife may be used for cutting, but use a metal ruler along the leading edge to help make certain that the leading edges of the balsa plank and of the cardboard pattern are exactly in line. This is advisable because of the length of the wing's leading edge. Also use the ruler to help keep the straight part of the trailing edge to an even line.

When the two wing pieces have been cut out, proceed as you did before and sand the wing pieces to exact shape. Be especially careful when sanding the wing tips and the curved section of the trailing edge near the center of the wings. Finish the job with fine sandpaper and lay one wing half on the other to check for accuracy. Sand down if necessary until both match.

The general shape of the aerofoil section of the main wing is shown on the plans marked C. Note that the bottom surface is flat, except for the rounded leading edge, and that the taper toward the trailing edge begins about 1½" in from the leading edge at section D. The aerofoil shape is rounded to a gentle curve, and this contour goes all along the wing. You can make yourself a template of cardboard or of thin aluminum in the shape of the top of the aerofoil and use this as a guide as you sand the wing down to its aerofoil.

When sanding the wing to its aerofoil shape, lay it on a flat surface after you have slightly rounded the bottom of the leading edge. This rounding should go back only about $\frac{1}{16}$" along the bottom, and come up at the front not more than $\frac{1}{32}$".

Begin to sand down to the aerofoil at section D and work toward the tip first, then toward the center from D. Get the over-all general shape first. If you have made a template, use it frequently as a check all along the wing half. Never try to sand down to the finished aerofoil shape at any one place. Do it as instructed. To emphasize this point, we repeat: *shape the aerofoil gradually all along the wing.*

When you are near enough to the correct aerofoil shape, with very fine sandpaper wrapped around a wood block or with an X-acto sandpaper holder sand the wing down to the exact contour of the aerofoil as shown on the plan as sections D and B.

Repeat the operation on the other wing half. *Make certain that one half has the aerofoil section on the side of the $\frac{1}{8}$" plank opposite to the one you made first.* One half is right and the other left, and if the two are made exactly alike you will have either two right or two left, and that is no good unless you want to make two gliders and then you will have to make two opposite halves anyway.

We can assume here that all the parts for the soaring glider are now completed. One more operation needs to be done before we can assemble the glider. A V-cut must be made in the top of the main wing mounting block. This V helps hold the dihedral to its proper angle. Note that the center of the V-cut is about $\frac{1}{16}$" deeper than the sides of the mounting block. When you cut this V-groove, keep a careful check on its depth. The cut can be made with a small X-acto razor saw. Sand the cut lightly to make it level and even-surfaced.

If you wish to fill in the pores of the balsa wood (this will strengthen the wood a little), you can now give all the parts of the glider a light spray with clear, model-paint spray, or brush on a coat of clear dope—the kind used for model airplanes. Allow this to soak in and dry over night. When dry, go over all parts with fine sandpaper until everything is smooth.

The next job is to obtain the proper dihedral in the wings. In order to do this, place both halves of the main wing on a level surface. Under the center where the wing halves join, place a bit of waxed paper about 6″ wide and 4″ long. This will keep glue from sticking to anything but the wings.

Put glue on the ends of the wing halves at the center. Allow the glue to dry for a short while, but not to harden. Push the wings together. Line up leading and trailing edges exactly, and then insert two wood blocks about 3″ long and 1″ square under the wing halves. Move the blocks in toward the center until the bottom of the wing tips is exactly 1¼″ above the working surface. Keep the wood blocks at right angles to the wings.

Insert pins at the center of the wing, if necessary, to keep it fastened down against the work board. Check the alignment and the height of the wings at the tips once more, and then allow to dry over night. When the glue has set and the wing can be raised from the workbench, take a piece of bedsheet and soak it with quick-drying glue. A strip 1¼″ wide and 2½″ long will do nicely. Place this at the center section for reinforcement. Allow to dry and then trim off with an X-acto blade, but avoid trimming off any of the leading or trailing edge. It may be necessary to use fine sandpaper in order to make the edges smooth. You may also have to fasten it down here and there with more glue.

The first step in assembly is to place the stabilizer on the rear of the fuselage, as shown on the drawings. Glue it in position and use a few small pins to keep it in place until dry. Check the alignment. It must be at right angles to the fuselage looking at it from the top and from the rear. If the stabilizer dips to either side, correct it before the glue dries, and remember that both wing tips must be exactly the same distance from the fuselage nose.

After the stabilizer has dried securely, the fin can be glued in position. Both leading edges, fin and stabilizer, must line up. Also check to see that the fin is pointing directly along the center line of the fuselage, and that it is exactly upright, not tilting to the right or the left. Small pins may be used, or cellophane tape, to hold it in position until the glue is dry. You can use a bit more glue here than you did to hold the stabilizer. Run some along either side of the fin and to the top of the stabilizer. Never use too much glue anywhere; try always to strike a happy medium, using just enough to hold securely and not enough to make a messy job of it.

The tail surfaces completed, it is now time to put on the main wing. To do this, it is best to prop up the fuselage between two heavy books laid along the fuselage so that the books are beneath the stabilizer as well as against the fuselage sides. When you have done that, put a good deal of cement into the V of the wing mounting block and allow it to get a bit tacky. Then place the main wing on the mounting block. Once again, with the wood blocks or with books, or anything that will hold them, prop up the wings at the tips so that they remain in position until the glue has dried. You *must* make certain that neither side of the wing dips downward while the glue is drying. Very carefully measure the height above your working surface and make sure that it remains the same. It is a good idea to let the glue dry overnight. Then run more glue between the bottom surface of each wing half and the wing mounting block.

You can insert a piano wire skid into the nose of the glider now, as shown on the plans. This will aid landings.

To test-fly the glider, try to find a place that lacks trees or any objects that the glider can smash into. You don't want to break it up before you have had your fun with it! If a field with tall grass can be found, so much the better. Even the beach is a good place to test it, but make sure that the wind is blowing away from the water.

If you have already hollowed out the nose, use modeling clay as ballast. Fill the hole a little at a time until you get enough weight to give a shallow glide downward. You may have to bend up the trailing edges of the stabilizer to get the proper glide. Wet them and then bend them up until your glide is smooth and long. If you cut off the glider's nose to provide a hollow, glue it back in place after the proper weight has been inserted in the hollow.

In case you did not cut off the glider's nose section, you can insert one or more nails into the nose until it is properly weighted. Of course, you may not want to weight the glider this way. You can fasten the weighing objects in place with cellophane tape, although this is not the best idea.

To get good flights, do not try to use this glider the way you did the stunt glider. Take it between the thumb and forefinger and, with the nose pointed very slightly downward, thrust it gently forward. The glider should take a long, sweeping, soaring flight, looking like a seagull as it flies.

Until you get this kind of flight, hand launched, the adjustments to be made have to do with the proper weight and the upward setting of the trailing edges of the stabilizer. Since no two gliders will be made exactly alike, each one must be individually adjusted by its builder. This is part of learning how to make a flying model work, the do-it-yourself method, and the best way of all.

If you are lucky enough to live in a place that has open spaces, either at the shore or inland, you can place a hook in the glider's nose (you don't use a skid in this case, and the hook may make it necessary to readjust the weight or stabilizer setting) and use a shock cord for launching the glider.

A word of warning is in order here. When the glider is launched by a shock cord, it gains altitude and may fly high enough and far enough away from you so that you will never see it again. A small typewritten piece of paper carrying your name, address and notice of reward if found and brought back to you should be glued to the glider.

To make a shock cord, about 3 feet of flat, model-airplane rubber is used. This is tied to about 6 feet of fishing line at one end and 1 foot of line at the other. At the end of the 1 foot of line, a ring is tied. This ring should be made of piano wire and be about 1" in diameter, with the ends of the loop overlapping and soldered together.

The wire loop or ring is placed on the hook in the glider's nose and both the hook and the ring are adjusted so that they will separate when the glider is just about vertical to the snap of the shock cord.

It takes two people to launch the glider. One holds the glider (between the thumb and forefinger, as usual) and the other takes the long end of the fishing line and, walking forward, pulls the line until the rubber band is stretched out about one and a half times its length. The person at the end of the shock line calls a "Let go!" to the one holding the glider and at the same time gives a sharp, extra tug at the line. Up goes the glider and the line drops away. A wonderful thrill is shared as the glider soars like a bird—gracefully, silently dipping and turning, and staying up for many minutes.

Chapter 5

The R.O.G.
Flying Model

Now that two different types of gliders have been built, it is time to turn to the powered model aircraft. The simplest is the R.O.G. The letters stand for Rise Off Ground and that is exactly what this model is capable of. Though it is a bit more complicated than an all-balsa-wood model, it is nevertheless easy to make and excellent results are always obtained.

The plans call for a model with a wingspread of 15″ and a length of 10$\frac{1}{16}$″ from propeller hanger to tail. You may cut all measurements in half to make a smaller airplane. You will observe when looking at the plans that the wings are made of lengths of balsa wood and are covered with light model-airplane tissue. Although the wings in this case are built up for lightness, they could be made of $\frac{1}{32}$″ sheet balsa, formed and sanded down exactly as were those of the soaring glider. However, the gain in lightness and, therefore, the better flying qualities of lighter wings that give good lift, make the added work well worth the effort.

For materials you will need two 3-foot lengths of $\frac{1}{8}$″ by $\frac{1}{16}$″ hard balsa for the leading and trailing edges, and the tips of the main wing. Two 3-foot lengths of $\frac{1}{16}$″-square hard balsa are needed for the wing ribs and the elevator. An 18″ length of $\frac{1}{16}$″ by $\frac{1}{32}$″ hard balsa will do to make the fin. The stick fuselage is made from hard balsa ⅛″ by ⅜″ by 10¹⁄₁₆″ long. One 3-foot length of ⅟₃₂″-diameter piano wire is needed, too.

The landing gear, the wire wing clips, the propeller shaft, and the rear hook of the rubber motor are made of piano wire. You can make the landing gear of bamboo ⅟₃₂″ in diameter, if you wish. The propeller, of either balsa wood or plastic, is 5⅝″ long. The wheels, 1″ in diameter, may be purchased or made of paper, as shown on the plans. Construction will be described later on. For the propeller hanger, a piece of ⅟₃₂″-thick aluminum 1¾″ long is used.

The first part of the R.O.G. to make is the fuselage—in this case, a single stick of balsa wood. You will note that it is tapered from the front and from the back to a center point about 4⅜″ in from the front where the full width of the ⅜″ wood is used.

Starting from the front and using a steel rule as a guide, measure down ³⁄₁₆″. Mark it and then make another mark 4⅜″ from the nose. Draw a pencil line. Then, from the 4⅜″ mark, make another mark with your pencil 4″ behind it and ¼″ down from the stick's upper edge. From the 4″ mark, draw a line so that it measures ³⁄₃₂″ wide at the tail. A glance at the drawing will guide you to these measurements.

Check the measurements and the pencil lines you have drawn on the fuselage stick. Now using the steel ruler as a guide, cut away the excess balsa wood, using your X-acto knife. Watch your fingers and work carefully and slowly. If you are not too certain, allow a little space between the pencil line and your cut and finish to your line with fine sandpaper, just as you did with the glider parts. When the stick has been shaped, go over it with fine sandpaper and make it smooth.

Now cut the piece of aluminum that you will use for the propeller hanger. This is ⅛″ wide. Bend it to shape following the dimensions given on the plans. Take your time here, for, though the bending is simple, you must be sure of your measurements. As guides, use the detail drawing and the side view showing the propeller hanger attached to the motor stick. When the hanger is bent to shape, make a ⅟₃₂″-diameter hole in the hanger, as shown. You can drill this out or force a hole through the soft aluminum with a steel scribe. Be careful that you do not bend the hanger out of shape while making the holes or punch a hole in your finger—a job all too easily done.

The propeller hanger should be filed down, using an X-acto flat file, so that the edges are all square and smooth. Place the propeller hanger on the front of the fuselage (motor) stick and hold it in position with quick-drying, clear glue. Also bind it to the fuselage stick by wrapping sewing thread around it so that the hanger extensions are pressed tightly against the top and the bottom of the fuselage stick. Wrap it with one full line of sewing thread, as shown. Knot the thread so that the ends do not come off. Cover the thread with glue and allow it to dry.

Bend the rear hook of the rubber motor out of $\frac{1}{32}$"-diameter piano wire, as shown in the details. However, note that the top part of the hook is not bent down until it has been inserted through the fuselage. This is done simply by working the piano wire hook into the wood until it comes out the top.

Then bend the wire over. Glue it to the fuselage and wrap some thread around it, just as you did with the propeller hanger. Glue the wrapped thread well and allow it to dry.

Be certain that you have made both the propeller hanger and the rear rubber hook long enough so that, when the rubber band used for the motive power is in place, the rubber will clear the fuselage stick at its deepest point, $4\frac{3}{8}$" back from the nose.

You have a choice of either $\frac{1}{32}$"-diameter bamboo or piano wire for the landing gear parts. Either will do. Their lengths are identical, but if bamboo is used it can be a little more than $\frac{1}{32}$" in diameter if you are looking for plenty of strength. Both the wire and the bamboo fasten to the fuselage stick at exactly the same place; namely, $\frac{1}{8}$" down from the top of the motor (fuselage) stick. The front strut goes about 1" back from the nose and the rear strut $2\frac{1}{2}$" back from the nose.

Although the bamboo can be simply glued in place, the tips of the landing gear struts, where they touch the fuselage stick, should be sandpapered to a slight point and carefully inserted into the sides of the fuselage stick just a bit for added strength. The bottom of the struts should be spread apart $2\frac{15}{16}$". An axle $3\frac{3}{4}$" long is glued where the struts join at the bottom. Make sure that you allow at least $\frac{3}{8}$" to stick out at each end of the axle beyond the bottom of the landing gear struts for the wheels to go on.

If you are going to use piano wire struts, each side should be made up from one length of wire bent into a long V. Cut it to length, as shown on the plan, and carefully insert it into the fuselage in the same way as described for the bamboo. Make certain to use enough glue to hold the struts securely to the fuselage stick. Check the spread and the length of the strut after you have put them in place. They must agree with the measurements on the plans, and must extend far enough so that, when the wheels are in place, the propeller clears the ground by at least $\frac{1}{2}$". Also, the struts must be back far enough so that the propeller, when it is revolving, does not hit the wheels. Clearance here should also be about $\frac{1}{2}$".

The axle of the wire landing gear is fixed to the bottom of the landing gear with thread and some glue. Fasten it securely and wrap each side with at least five turns of heavy sewing thread. Spread a good amount of glue over the thread. Make certain that the axle allows ⅜″ on each side where the wheels go on.

When the landing gear has dried, you can put the wheels in place. If you have not purchased wheels 1″ in diameter, then you can make a very strong and light pair out of heavy writing paper. They are very easy to construct. On writing paper draw four circles 1¹⁄₁₆″ in diameter. Cut out the circles, using great care. The circles must be absolutely round or the finished wheel will bump and jump all over the place.

Now make a cut from the rim of your circle, or disk, to the center. Overlap the cut by pulling the disk together just about ½″. The disk will take on a cone shape. Put some glue between the paper overlap and allow it to dry thoroughly. You now have one cone-shaped side of the wheel. Repeat this process three more times. Then you have four separate cones. Carefully glue two cones together for each wheel. With a long pin, check to see that the centers are in line, and arrange the overlaps so that they are placed one up on one side of the wheel and one down on the other side of the wheel. While the glue is still wet, spin the wheel around a pin inserted for a test axle at the wheel's center. It should run true and not wobble. If the glue is wet enough, you can adjust the wheel so that it will run true. You may have to make several wheels until you get two that are good enough to use. But don't let this stop you. Try for as much perfection as possible.

When the wheels have been constructed successfully, small metal washers with a center hole ¹⁄₃₂″ in diameter, to take either a wire or a bamboo axle, are glued to the sides of the wheels at the center. Be careful not to fill up the center holes of the washers with glue, but use plenty to secure them to the wheels firmly. Four are needed, and they can be obtained, in brass, at your model shop. Put the wheels on the axle after the glue on the washers is dry. Place a drop of glue at the axle ends to keep the wheels from coming off. The wheels must run freely, so be careful with the glue.

Purchase the propeller at your model store in plastic or wood. Wood is lighter in weight but the plastic is almost unbreakable.

Through the propeller's center, insert a wire shaft and hook made in one piece from a length of ¹⁄₃₂″-diameter wire. Bend the hook to shape with a flat-nosed pliers. Remember to make the shaft long enough so that you have enough wire to bend over the propeller. The shaft should be not less than ¾″ from the front of the hook forward.

Insert the shaft through the propeller hanger as shown in the detail sketches. Place one or two small brass washers with a ¹⁄₃₂″-diameter hole over the shaft and then slip on the propeller. Make certain that the back of the propeller clears the hanger. Add washers if it is necessary to make it do so. Very carefully, so that you do not damage anything, bend the shaft that extends beyond the propeller hub, over the propeller to form a hook, as indicated on the plans. If this assembly has been constructed properly, the propeller should turn freely and evenly without wobble when you blow at the propeller. If wobble is present, you will have to find the cause, such as a hole in the hanger that does not line up, a bent shaft or an improperly made hook. The hook should be no more than ¼" from top to bottom where it takes the rubber.

When you have checked the propeller units, take a 17" length of ⅛", flat, model-airplane rubber and tie the ends together securely. Place the front end of the rubber loop over the propeller hook and the knotted end over the rear hook. The motor power is now in your R.O.G. A couple of winds of the propeller to the right, when facing it, will pull the fuselage along the table. This is for test purposes, and on no account should you wind up the rubber more than just a few turns—just enough to see that it works well.

Now let's turn to the elevator. One half of the elevator is shown on the plans. Since both sides are the same, simply double the plans over to make the entire wing, just as you did with the gliders. The elevator is made up of ¹⁄₁₆"-square, hard balsa wood. Lay out the plan on a smooth, flat surface. Place waxed paper over the plan and outline the elevator's leading and trailing edges with long pins. Cut your ¹⁄₁₆"-square wood to the lengths of the elevator's leading and trailing edges. The trailing edge is 6¼" long and the leading edge is 5¾" long. Between them go two ¹⁄₁₆"-square ribs placed 1½" out from the center. Each wing tip is also made of ¹⁄₁₆"-square balsa wood. However, there is a center rib which is made from a scrap piece of 1" by ¹⁄₁₆" wood. This is for added strength and for a base for bracing against the bottom back of the fuselage stick.

See that you get a good amount of quick-drying glue at all joints, without being sloppy about it. Allow the unit to dry, and while it is doing so, make up the fin. Once again lay waxed paper over your plan. Outline the fin with pins and make up the framework of ¹⁄₁₆" by ¹⁄₃₂" hard balsa wood. This is a simple structure having a leading edge and a trailing edge, a top and a bottom.

The last part to be made is the main wing. This is built up over the plan, using waxed paper between the wood and the plan. Everything should be outlined with pins in order to keep the parts in their proper places.

The leading and trailing edges and the wing tips are all made of hard balsa wood measuring ¹⁄₁₆" by ⅛". The four ribs are ¹⁄₁₆" square and the two center ribs measure ¼" by ¹⁄₁₆".

Measuring out from the center, the ¹⁄₁₆"-square ribs are placed at the ¾" mark for the inner set and at the 4" mark for the outer set.

At the center line go the two ¼" by ⅟₁₆" pieces as shown on the plans.

Use enough glue to make certain that all the ribs, leading and trailing edges, and wing tips cement together securely. As you did with the gliders, make each side of the main wing separately, but do not worry about right and left when putting them together, for both are exactly the same.

When all of the structures of the flying surfaces are dry—elevator, fin, and the halves of the main wing—they are ready to be covered. The covering is the lightest-weight model-airplane tissue you can find at your model shop. One sheet should be enough, for it.is found usually in sheets 24" or more square.

Just to make sure that you get the hang of covering model-airplane wings, if you have never done it before, do the easy job first . . . put the paper on the fin.

First cut out a square of paper measuring about 3" by 4". Then coat one side of the fin frame with watered-down Elmer's glue, applied with a brush. Hold the paper tight and lay it over the fin frame so that it touches the trailing edge first. Then very carefully pull it so that it stretches over the rest of the framework without wrinkles. You can make up a fake frame of balsa wood and practice on that until you get the hang of it, if you do not want to chance it right away. Keep your fingers free of glue or you will run into trouble.

The fin is covered on one side only; it does not matter which. We are not concerned with the study of aerodynamics in this model, so either side will do.

Both the elevator and the halves of the main wing are covered in the same manner as the fin, although these are a little more difficult to work with. They are covered on top only. Make certain that there is a right and a left to the main wing, with the covering being placed on top. Use a watered-down mixture of Elmer's glue applied with a soft brush on all wing frames. You might try to do the job on the main wing a little at a time, brushing on the glue just before the paper is laid on the wood frame. However, you will soon learn what method best suits you. You must have a wrinkle-free covering that is tight enough not to sag and flop. Minor pulls and a small wrinkle near an edge are all right, but good clean work should always be seriously tried for. Cut out your tissue pieces about 1" larger than you need and trim off the excess, when the covering has dried, with sharp scissors or an X-acto knife.

Make sure that the wings do not warp, twist, or otherwise get out of shape. It is a good idea to pin down the flying surfaces to a flat board or table top, over waxed paper, so that each unit is perfectly flat all around until dry. Do not attempt to use a book or similar object to hold the flying surfaces flat, for the glue will stick to the book, right through the tissue covering, and there go your wings! Allow them to dry over night.

In the meantime, make up two main wing clips. These are alike and are bent out of $\frac{1}{32}$"-diameter wire, using flat-nosed pliers. The length of the bends will be found in the detailed sketches. Bend back the $\frac{3}{8}$" ends of the two clips. These bent-back ends are to be glued to the bottom of the leading and trailing edges of the main wing after it is joined together. Test for a snug fit on the fuselage stick. Adjust if necessary.

In order to produce the proper dihedral or upward tilt of the main wing, glue the centers together, making certain that leading and trailing edges are exactly in line. While the glue is still wet, raise both ends of the wing with the wooden blocks placed below them, or with two books, until the tips measure $2\frac{7}{16}$" above your working surface. Hold down the center so that the wings maintain their upward tilt. Be sure that leading and trailing edges are exactly level and that neither is higher or lower than the other at the tips. In short, give the wing its dihedral angle in exactly the same way as you did with the glider models. Allow the main wing to dry over night.

Now you can glue the elevator to the bottom of the fuselage stick. Make sure that the elevator is square to the fuselage stick and at right angles to it. One side of the leading edge should not be farther front than the other, nor should one wing tip be higher than the other if checked against the fuselage (motor) stick.

When the elevator has dried in place, glue the fin to the top rear of the fuselage. Check it for positive line-up forward, and be certain that it does not tilt toward either side. Use small pins carefully placed to hold it upright until dry.

The main wing should be ready for the wing clips now. They are, as mentioned before, glued to the bottom of the wing where they touch the leading and trailing edges, as shown on the plans. Use enough glue to hold them securely in place. Above all, see that they line up exactly when viewing them from the front.

Now fit the wing, by the clips, to the fuselage stick. Always press the wing on gently, using your first two fingers placed over the ends of the wing clips where they touch the wing. Never try to position the wing by pressing at any other place, or you will surely break the wing into two or more useless pieces. Now the model is finished.

The next step is to adjust it so that it flies properly. Place your fingers below the center of the wing tips. The plane should nose down very gently. If it dips down at the nose heavily, move the wing forward. If the tail dips downward, move the wing backward. When the nose just about drops downward, the wing is in the correct place.

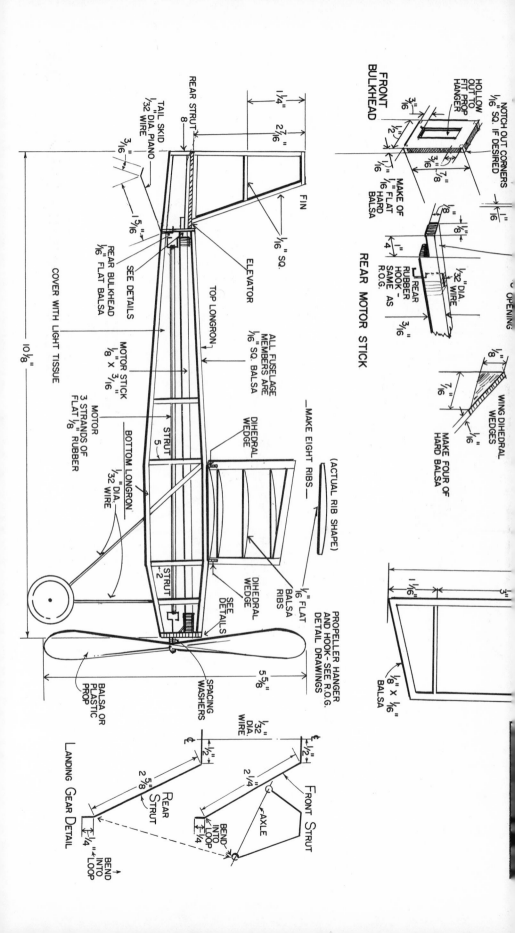

FRONT BULKHEAD

NOTCH OUT CORNERS
1/16" SQ. IF DESIRED

HOLLOW
OUT TO
FIT PROP
HANGER

3/16"

1/2"

3/16"

1/16"

1/16"

7/8"

MAKE OF
1/16" FLAT HARD
BALSA

OPENING

REAR MOTOR STICK

1/8"

1/8"

1/4"

1/32" DIA.
WIRE

REAR
RUBBER
HOOK –
SAME AS
R.O.G.

3/16"

1/8"

7/16"

1/16"

1/16"

WING DIHEDRAL
WEDGES

MAKE FOUR OF
HARD BALSA

REAR STRUT
8

TAIL SKID
1/32" DIA. PIANO
WIRE

3/16"

1 5/16"

REAR BULKHEAD
1/16" FLAT BALSA

SEE DETAILS

COVER WITH LIGHT TISSUE

10 1/8"

1 1/4"

2 7/16"

FIN

1/16" SQ.

ELEVATOR

TOP LONGRON

ALL FUSELAGE
MEMBERS ARE
1/16" SQ. BALSA

MOTOR STICK
1/8" x 3/16"

BOTTOM LONGRON
1/32" WIRE

MOTOR
3 STRANDS OF
FLAT 1/8" RUBBER

STRUT
5

STRUT
2

DIHEDRAL
WEDGE

DIHEDRAL
WEDGE

SEE DETAILS

– MAKE EIGHT RIBS –

(ACTUAL RIB SHAPE)

1/16" FLAT
BALSA RIBS

PROPELLER HANGER
AND HOOK- SEE R.O.G.
DETAIL DRAWINGS

BALSA OR
PLASTIC
PROP

SPACING
WASHERS

5 5/8"

1 1/16"

3"

1/8" x 1/16"
BALSA

Rear Strut

1/32" DIA.
WIRE

1/2"

2 5/8"

1/4"

BEND
INTO LOOP

Front Strut

1/2"

2 1/4"

AXLE

BEND
INTO
LOOP

1/4"

BEND
INTO LOOP

Landing Gear Detail

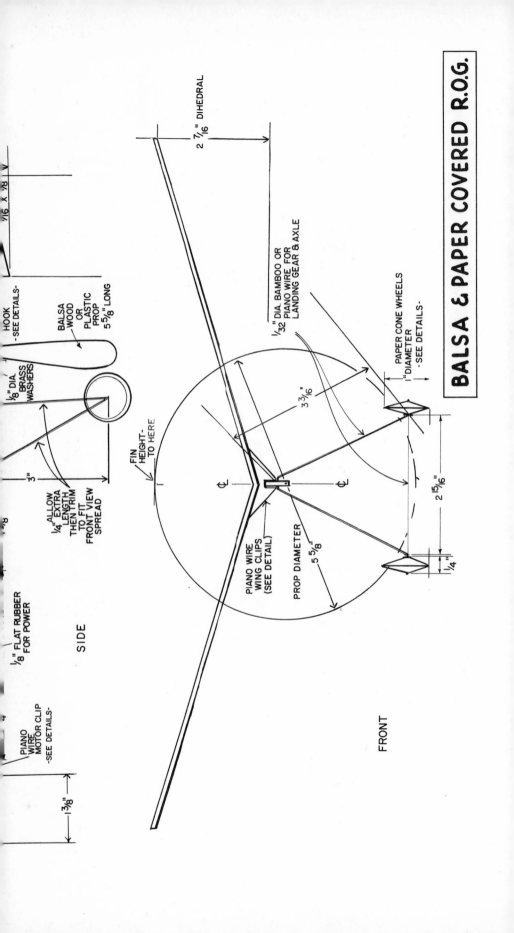

BALSA & PAPER COVERED R.O.G.

SIDE

FRONT

2 7/16" DIHEDRAL

1/16 x 7/8

HOOK
- SEE DETAILS-

BALSA WOOD OR PLASTIC PROP 5 5/8" LONG

1/8" DIA. BRASS WASHERS

3"

ALLOW 1/4" EXTRA LENGTH THEN TRIM TO FIT FRONT VIEW SPREAD

1/8" FLAT RUBBER FOR POWER

PIANO WIRE MOTOR CLIP -SEE DETAILS-

1 3/8"

FIN HEIGHT- TO HERE

PIANO WIRE WING CLIPS (SEE DETAIL)

PROP DIAMETER 5 5/8"

1/16" DIA. BAMBOO OR 1/32 PIANO WIRE FOR LANDING GEAR & AXLE

3 3/16"

PAPER CONE WHEELS 1" DIAMETER -SEE DETAILS-

2 15/16"

1/4"

CL

CL

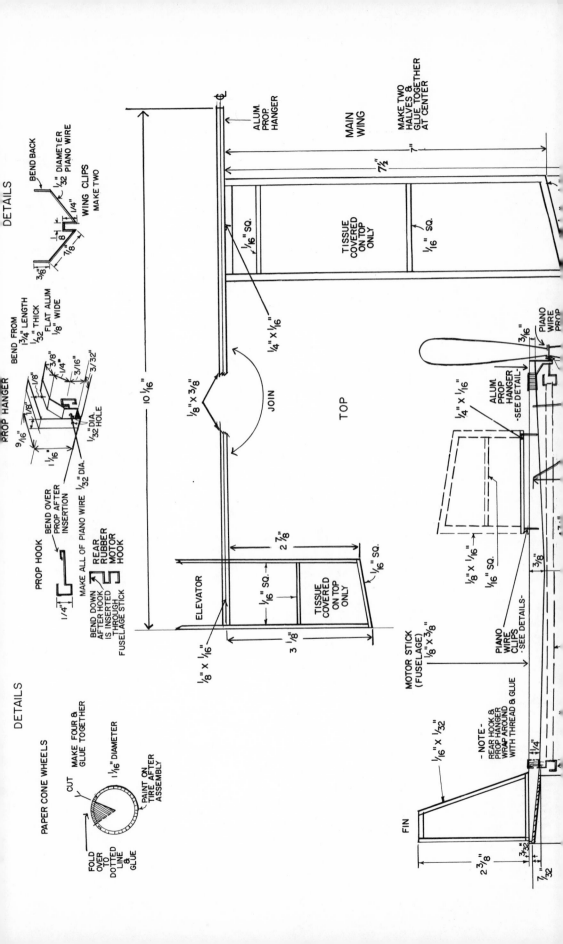

DETAILS

BEND BACK

$\frac{1}{32}$" DIAMETER PIANO WIRE

WING CLIPS
MAKE TWO

$\frac{1}{4}$"

$\frac{1}{8}$"

$\frac{1}{8}$"

$\frac{3}{8}$"

$\frac{7}{8}$"

ALUM. PROP. HANGER

MAIN WING

MAKE TWO HALVES & GLUE TOGETHER AT CENTER

7"

$7\frac{1}{2}$"

$\frac{1}{16}$" SQ.

TISSUE COVERED ON TOP ONLY

$\frac{1}{16}$" SQ.

$\frac{1}{4}$" x $\frac{1}{16}$"

PROP HANGER

BEND FROM $1\frac{3}{4}$" LENGTH $\frac{1}{32}$" THICK FLAT ALUM. $\frac{1}{8}$" WIDE

$9\frac{1}{16}$"

$1\frac{1}{16}$"

$\frac{1}{8}$"

$\frac{1}{8}$"

$\frac{3}{8}$"

$\frac{1}{4}$"

$\frac{3}{16}$"

$\frac{3}{32}$"

$\frac{1}{32}$" DIA. HOLE

BEND OVER PROP AFTER INSERTION

$\frac{1}{32}$" DIA.

MAKE ALL OF PIANO WIRE

PROP HOOK

$\frac{1}{4}$"

BEND DOWN AFTER HOOK IS INSERTED THROUGH FUSELAGE STICK

REAR RUBBER MOTOR HOOK

$10\frac{1}{16}$"

$\frac{1}{8}$" x $\frac{3}{8}$"

JOIN

TOP

$2\frac{7}{8}$"

$\frac{1}{16}$" SQ.

TISSUE COVERED ON TOP ONLY

ELEVATOR

$\frac{1}{16}$" SQ.

$3\frac{1}{8}$"

$\frac{1}{8}$" x $\frac{1}{16}$"

PIANO WIRE PROP

$\frac{3}{16}$"

$\frac{1}{4}$" x $\frac{1}{16}$"

ALUM PROP HANGER
-SEE DETAIL-

$\frac{1}{8}$" x $\frac{1}{16}$"

$\frac{1}{16}$" SQ.

$\frac{3}{8}$"

MOTOR STICK (FUSELAGE) $\frac{1}{8}$" x $\frac{3}{8}$"

PIANO WIRE CLIPS
-SEE DETAILS-

DETAILS

PAPER CONE WHEELS

CUT

MAKE FOUR & GLUE TOGETHER

$1\frac{1}{16}$" DIAMETER

PAINT ON TIRE AFTER ASSEMBLY

FOLD OVER TO DOTTED LINE & GLUE

$\frac{1}{16}$" x $\frac{1}{32}$"

- NOTE -
REAR HOOK & PROP HANGER WRAP AROUND WITH THREAD & GLUE

$\frac{1}{4}$"

FIN

$2\frac{3}{8}$"

$\frac{3}{32}$"

$\frac{7}{32}$"

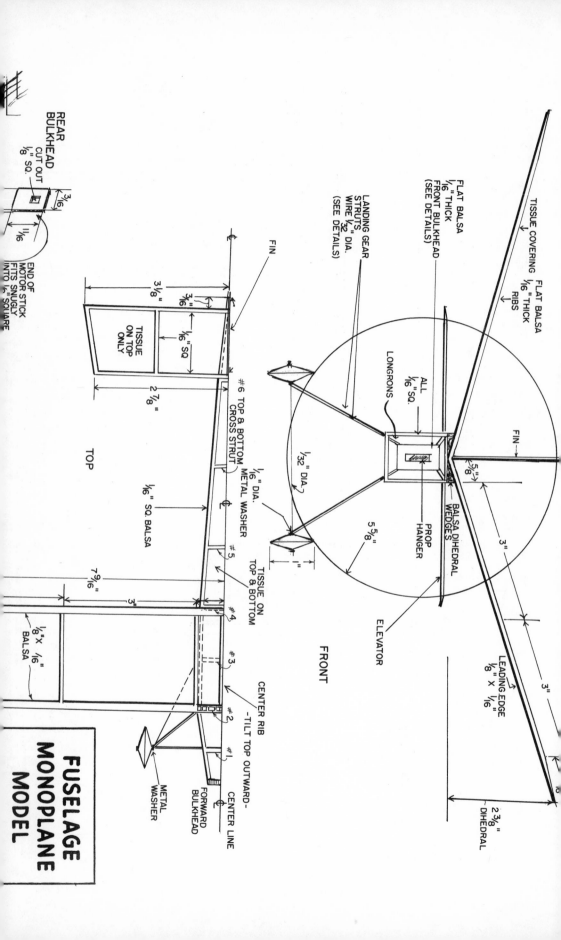

FUSELAGE MONOPLANE MODEL

Now find a place that is clear and free from obstacles and test-glide the model. It should glide gently forward. You may also test it by placing the wheels on the ground, lifting the tail with a finger and giving the model a gentle push forward. It should hop off the ground evenly and settle back.

For the first flight, wind up the propeller, turning it to the right as you face the model, until one complete row of knots appears in the rubber. Then you may either hand launch it or let it rise off the ground.

For hand launching, take the model between the thumb and forefinger, just in back of the rear landing gear strut. Allow the propeller to unwind a few turns and very gently thrust the plane forward with the nose tilted very slightly up.

For ground launching, hold the tip of the propeller with the thumb and forefinger of the left hand and raise the tail so that the plane is almost horizontal. The nose should be slightly upward. The thumb and forefinger of the right hand are used to hold the top of the fin. Gently thrust the plane forward after letting the propeller turn a few times. The plane should take off and rise gently, then glide to a good landing on its wheels.

If the plane noses forward, move the wing forward. You may not have placed it correctly for flying. If it noses up, move the wing back. Different angles may be obtained in the main wing by moving the wing clips up or down, front or rear; and by using these as adjustments, various kinds of flights can be made, including steep climbs and shallow glides. But that is what this is all about—an R.O.G. that will give you practice and teach you how to adjust and to fly a powered model successfully.

Chapter 6

The Fuselage Monoplane Model

The fuselage monoplane is almost exactly like the R.O.G., except that it has a full fuselage instead of a stick, and carries its wing atop the fuselage. Our model of the fuselage monoplane uses similar parts, such as the main wing, fin, elevator and fuselage stick (now called the motor stick), wheels and propeller.

Now we will make a fuselage, a new landing gear, and ribs for the wing. Having experience in the construction of the R.O.G. will make the building of the more difficult fuselage model much easier.

You will note several improvements in the fuselage model. For one thing, the flat "ribs" are now replaced with true ribs that actually have form. Since the fuselage adds weight to the plane, we now use three strands of rubber instead of two. The main wing is mounted directly on top of the fuselage and the dihedral is held to its angle by wood wedges instead of wire clips. At the rear bottom of the fuselage is a piano wire tail skid. Both the elevator and the fin are now mounted atop the fuselage. The struts of the landing gear are different and are fastened to the cross-members of the bottom of the fuselage instead of to a fuselage stick.

It is a good idea to look at the plans of both the R.O.G. and the fuselage model. Study them and compare them. See for yourself how this model evolved from the earlier design and what changes were necessary. It should be mentioned that the fuselage model follows, generally, the construction of most flying-model airplanes, either scratch-built or from kits, and that after the successful completion of this model you should be able to construct any other flying model. Any changes from this fuselage model would only be in design, size, and details.

Materials needed for the fuselage, fin and elevator are six 36" lengths of $\frac{1}{16}$"-square hard balsa wood, which should be enough with some left over just in case. One piece of $\frac{1}{16}$" flat, hard balsa is needed for the wing ribs, front and rear bulkheads, and wing dihedral wedges. About 18" should be enough. A 3-foot length or two of $\frac{1}{8}$" by $\frac{1}{16}$" hard balsa wood will be required for the leading and trailing ends, and for the tips of the main wing.

You will also need about 36" of $\frac{1}{32}$" diameter piano wire for the landing gear, propeller hook, rear rubber hook, and tail skid, a sheet of lightweight covering tissue, 24" square, and about 28" of flat, $\frac{1}{8}$" rubber for the motive power.

Since the propeller, the propeller hanger and the wheels are exactly the same as those of the R.O.G., consult the plans for the R.O.G. for material and details. This is an excellent place to explain that the rear of the motor stick, while having exactly the same type of rear, wire motor hook, is now cut to fit into the opening made in the rear bulkhead. But the construction and the fastening of the aluminum propeller hanger are exactly the same as for the R.O.G.

Now that you have some idea of the changes of design and your list of materials, you can start to build the model.

By now you have the idea and know what method you yourself like best. Lay out your plan sheet, or sheets, on a flat surface. Cover them with waxed paper and see that your balsa, pins, X-acto knife and glue are at hand.

Lay one of the $\frac{1}{16}$"-square strips over the drawing at the *top* longeron. Cut it to length. Notice that the longeron, at the rear, is fitted into the upper notch of the rear bulkhead. See the detail here. However, you may just butt it against the rear bulkhead if you wish, but then the longeron must be made $\frac{1}{16}$" shorter. Where the top longeron bends downward at the number 2 strut, you may have to notch the longeron's bottom surface, where it touches, in order to obtain the correct angle.

Place pins alongside the top and bottom of the longeron in order to hold it securely in position over the plan. Make certain that your pins do not get in the way of the upright struts. Also note that the rear of the top longerons on which the elevator lies are not attached to the fuselage until later, although they should be cut to length now.

The forward and rear bulkheads, like the rear lengths of the upper fuselage, are not put in place until later. However, now is the time to cut out all the rest of the side fuselage struts. There are eight of them. Numbers 1, 3, and 4 brace the landing gear. Number 4 strut is placed at an angle in order to carry the shock from the landing gear when the plane lands.

Now cut all the struts. Measure them by placing the end of the 1/16"-square wood tight up against the upper longeron. Then cut off each one exactly and squarely where each touches the top of the *bottom* longeron. Make two of each, 16 in all. One set of 8 is for the right side of the fuselage, and one set for the left side. Number each set 1 through 8 so that you will know where each one goes.

Next, cut the bottom longeron to its proper length. Place it over the plan. You may have to notch, or cut, the longeron where it touches strut number 3 and strut number 6 in order to give it the proper bend. Do this carefully, and then, with pins placed alongside the bottom longeron's top and bottom, hold it in position over the plan. Do not place the pins in a position where they will interfere with the struts.

Once the bottom longeron is in position, glue each of the struts in place. If you have been careful and have correctly marked them, they will fit right into place. Be sure that there is enough glue to hold the struts to the longerons without making a messy job of it. Allow the structure to dry thoroughly. Then very carefully remove the pins and lift the fuselage side off the plans. Be very careful that you do not break the wood. If, by some chance, any of the joints are not secure, add glue to them at this time.

In order to make the other side of the fuselage, it is necessary to repeat the operation that you have just completed. Put pins back in the same holes, through a new sheet of waxed paper. Try out the top longeron. Make certain that it is in exactly the same place as the one before it. Check its position by laying the completed fuselage side on top of it. Position and bend should be the same. Put the bottom longeron in place, and then add the upright struts. Before you glue anything, check again by placing the completed fuselage side against the new one. They should match exactly. If not, adjust until they do. Then glue the struts permanently to the longerons. Allow everything to dry thoroughly. Lift the side off the plan carefully after you remove the pins. Remember that all uprights, except number 4, must be at right angles (square) to the longerons.

Now cut to length the bottom and top cross-struts of the fuselage. Both bottom and top struts are exactly the same length where they fit in the fuselage. Make two of each, then mark them so that you know where they go. There are 12 struts. Since the drawing shows only half the top and bottom of the fuselage, you will have to use the following measurements as guides to their lengths. Number 1 is ⅝" long, numbers 2, 3, and 4 are ⅞" long; number 5 is ¾" long; number 6 is ½" long. From number 6 to the rear, the fuselage tapers until both number 8 struts touch.

Glue the fuselage together at its rear. Place glue on the inside of the right and left fuselage number 8 struts, and hold them together by wrapping some string about them. Let the fuselage rest on a flat surface until it is dry; however, it is a good idea to place the top and bottom number 6 cross-strut in position, without glue, in order to make certain that the proper rear taper is obtained while the glue is drying.

When the glue at the rear of the fuselage has dried, you can glue number 6 top and bottom struts in place, working from the rear forward. Check by looking down the fuselage to see that they are square and in exactly the same position. Allow the glue to dry. It should be mentioned here that the fuselage should be placed upright on a smooth surface while the top and bottom struts are drying in position, and a constant check should be made in order to make sure that the fuselage is absolutely square and without twists down its entire length. You can use wooden blocks or hard-cover books as aids in holding the fuselage together while the glue is drying.

When number 6 top and bottom struts have dried, then proceed to put number 5, top and bottom, in place. Glue securely, and when the glue is dry, add top and bottom number 4. You will see that from the number 4 struts forward to strut number 2 the fuselage is straight on both sides; and from number 2, it tapers inward in order to match the forward bulkhead.

Put numbers 4, 3, and 2 in place. Bend the longerons top and bottom so that they press against the three struts, then glue the struts in place and hold the fuselage sides with a book or wooden block propped against them so that they do not spring apart until the glue has thoroughly dried.

You may have to cut or notch the four longerons in order to make the taper in the front of the fuselage. See the top view on the plans. However, with a lot of care, you may be able to bend the longerons so they will take the number 1 strut, top and bottom. However you do it, just make certain that when the struts have been glued in position they all line up right down the fuselage. A square fuselage is a necessity.

Now you have a fuselage that, in order to be complete, needs a front bulkhead, a rear bulkhead and two top longerons for the tail assembly to sit on.

Both front and rear bulkheads are made of 1/16" flat, hard balsa wood. It is a good idea first to draw the outline of both bulkheads on the balsa-wood sheet. (Measurements and details will be found on the drawings.)

Before you cut the bulkheads, however, cut out their centers. By so doing you will not split the wood. You will see that the rear bulkhead has an interior opening only ⅛″ square, and that the forward bulkhead has a larger opening which is made to fit the width and length of the aluminum propeller hanger. The propeller hanger should fit snugly into the opening in the forward bulkhead. Since each modeler will make an opening that will be slightly different from others, no hard-and-fast measurements can be given. You must fit your hanger to the opening you make in the bulkhead.

When the two bulkhead openings have been carefully cut out with your X-acto knife, sandpaper the openings smooth. Now cut the outside outline. Do this carefully, for you do not want the wood to split apart. Use a steel straightedge, or ruler, to guide you. Your bulkhead must have top and sides at right angles to each other—in other words, it must be *square*.

Place the rear bulkhead in position first. It may be necessary to cut notches, ¹⁄₁₆″ square, in the four corners of the bulkhead in order to have it fit the fuselage longerons correctly. Make certain that the rear bulkhead does not force the longerons apart even slightly, and that it is in exactly the correct place, 1⅝″ forward of the rear number 8 strut. Check to see that it is at right angles to all the fuselage members, and if necessary you can then trim off the sides or the top and bottom. Glue the rear bulkhead in place. When the glue has dried, attach the two upper rear longerons to the fuselage. These butt against the rear of the bulkhead and are set in place ⅛″ below the main top longerons as shown in the drawings. This completes the rear of the fuselage.

The forward bulkhead is first checked for squareness, then sandpapered smooth all around, and set against the front of the four longerons. The bulkhead must fit the height and the width of the fuselage, where the members touch it. If they do not, you will have to sand the bulkhead down until it does. You may make it butt against the front of the four longerons, or you may notch the four corners out ¹⁄₁₆″ square and fit it over the longerons. Check before you glue it permanently in place, and make certain that it is square and lines up with the rest of the fuselage upright and the cross-struts. Then glue it securely.

In order to make the rubber motor, a motor stick must be made. It consists of a piece of hard balsa ⅛″ by ³⁄₁₆″. The rear of the motor stick is cut down to ⅛″ square, as shown on the detail drawings. This ⅛″-square notch fits into the ⅛″-square opening in the rear bulkhead. At the forward end of the motor stick, the propeller hanger is attached with glue and one wrapping of fine thread. Be careful when you wrap the thread that you put it on evenly, otherwise it will prevent the propeller hanger from fitting properly into the opening in the forward bulkhead. If, by some chance, it does not fit, you will have to sand out the opening carefully to allow the hanger to go past and fit as it should. The front rubber motor hook is also the propeller shaft. It is run through the hanger and fastened to the propeller. Put spacing washers between the propeller and the hanger as you did with the R.O.G. The rear rubber hook is also made like that of the R.O.G., but in this case you must make certain that it is put in position far enough forward so that, when the rubber is attached to it, nothing touches the rear bulkhead.

The motor stick is designed to come out of the fuselage. It is simpler to wind up the motor when it is removed; also, in case the rubber breaks when winding, it will not destroy the model. The motor stick prevents the strain of tightly wound rubber from affecting the fuselage. If the motor stick tends to come out by itself, a pin can be driven through a hole drilled through the forward bulkhead and the motor stick, where they touch. This will hold everything in place. The pin, a short length of $\frac{1}{32}$"-diameter wire, must be made so that it can be pulled out when the motor stick is to be removed.

Glued to the bottom center and front of the rear bulkhead is the tail skid. It holds the rear of the plane off the ground. Bend it out of $\frac{1}{32}$"-diameter piano wire to the length shown: $\frac{3}{16}$" for the foot, $1\frac{5}{16}$" for the arm, and $\frac{1}{4}$" for the bend upward that goes against the bulkhead. Glue the tail skid securely in place.

The landing gear is made entirely of $\frac{1}{32}$"-diameter piano wire. Bend a front strut and a rear strut, as shown on the plan and in the details.

The legs of the front landing gear struts are $2\frac{5}{8}$" long, and the bend that fits below the fuselage against number 1 cross-strut is 1" wide. The $\frac{1}{4}$" extra length at the bottom of each of the struts is bent into a loop with a pair of round-nosed pliers so that the axle, also of $\frac{1}{32}$"-diameter wire, can fit through it. It can be a loose fit.

The legs of the rear landing gear strut are $2\frac{1}{4}$" long and the bend where it fits below cross fuselage strut number 3 is 1" wide. The bottom $\frac{1}{4}$" extra length is bent into a loop like that of the front member.

The axle of $\frac{1}{32}$"-diameter wire is 4" long and goes through the loops at the bottom of the landing gear struts, as previously explained.

The wheels, made of paper, are constructed in exactly the same way as those of the R.O.G. But you may purchase them if you wish. They are 1" in diameter.

Glue the front landing gear strut to the bottom of cross-strut number 1. Use enough glue to hold it securely, and then, if you wish, you can bind it with fine sewing thread, also lightly gone over with glue. The rear landing gear strut is fastened to the fuselage in the same way as the front strut. See to it that it tilts forward so that the loops at the bottom of front and rear struts match. The axle goes through them. It is a good idea to insert the axle through the loops while the axle is drying. This will assure that the struts are in proper relation to each other. The front strut must remain straight up and down with the rear strut slanting forward to it.

You can make the wheels yourself. They consist of four cones of heavy writing paper, made and glued together in exactly the same way as those you made for the R.O.G. Do not forget to place a small metal washer at each side of the center of the wheels where the axle goes through. The washer centers should be $\frac{1}{32}''$ in diameter to take the axle. Glue the wheels to each side of the axle, as shown on the plans. The loops should be large enough to let the axle roll freely and the wheels should be just far enough away from the loops and the landing gear struts so that they also revolve freely. Take care that the wheels do not interfere with the propeller. They must be back far enough to clear the propeller by at least $\frac{1}{8}''$ to $\frac{1}{4}''$. The washers placed between the propeller and the propeller hanger are also there to provide this clearance.

Put some rubber strands over the propeller hanger hook and the rear hook, turn the propeller to the right, and wind up the rubber a few times. The motor stick is then inserted into the fuselage. Let the propeller go, and if all is in order the fuselage will move forward freely. Now is the time to make any corrections that are necessary.

Now that the fuselage is completed, the flying surfaces are made. Begin with the fin.

Put a piece of waxed paper over the plan of the fin. Cut the $\frac{1}{16}''$-square balsa wood to the length of the tip, the trailing and leading edges, and the bottom. Lay the pieces over the plan and glue the frame of the fin together. Add the center brace and hold everything in position with pins until dry.

While the fin is drying, you can make the elevator. Like the fin, it is made up of $\frac{1}{16}''$-square balsa wood. Since it is made in one piece, the plans will have to be doubled, so that you have both right and left sides of the elevator joining. Simply draw two layouts and join them at the center line. Make certain that the $3\frac{1}{8}''$-long trailing edge is at the rear of both sides.

Lay the balsa wood over the waxed paper covering your plans. Now cut all the parts to size. The ribs go $1\frac{1}{2}''$ out from the elevator's center line. Hold the assembly together with pins until the glue is thoroughly dry.

Although the outline of the main wing is like that of the R.O.G., the wing is different because it has, as mentioned, true ribs in place of square stock. The rib shape is to be found on the drawing. Make a rib pattern either of cardboard or, best of all, of metal. You will see that the design of the rib is simple.

Using your pattern, cut eight ribs out of $\frac{1}{16}''$ flat, hard balsa wood. Lay them all together and with fine sandpaper smooth them down *all at once,* so that they have the same curve. Height and length must be exactly the same for all ribs.

While you have some of the $\frac{1}{16}''$ flat balsa wood on hand, you can cut out the four dihedral wing wedges. The plan details will show you how they look and give you the measurements. Like the ribs, these wedges must all be exactly the same, so make them carefully. Cut them out with your X-acto knife and sand them smooth with very fine sandpaper. You can make them by using a metal pattern, or you can mark them out directly on the balsa wood. A steel straightedge should be used as a guide when laying them out as well as when cutting them, even if you see a pattern.

The leading and trailing edges of the main wing and the wing tips are made of $\frac{1}{8}''$ by $\frac{1}{16}''$ hard balsa wood. Make up your full-size plan, and remember that the main wing is made in two pieces, one right and the other left. Construct each half separately. This is done because of the dihedral angle of the wings.

You can make two individual pieces on your drawing, or one to be separated at the center line. However you do it, you must have a right and a left side. Check yourself against mistakes by laying the trailing edges down first. Each side's trailing edge is $7\frac{9}{16}''$ long. Over the waxed paper which should cover your plan, hold the trailing edge in position with pins. Make certain that the pins will not interfere with the placement of the wing ribs.

Now put the leading edges on the plan and hold them in place with pins. Next add the wing tips. Glue them to the leading and trailing edges. Hold them in place with pins until the glue is dry. Then, with a good amount of glue, put each of the ribs in position. Make certain that they fit snugly between the leading and trailing edges, but do not force them into position. Sandpaper off the ends, if necessary, to make them fit properly. Use at least four evenly spaced pins to hold each rib. They all must be at right angles to the working surface, except the center ribs, which slant outward to take the dihedral angle.

When the flying surfaces are finished and you have carefully removed them from the work board, and after all the pins have been removed, go over the frames to see that no little lumps of glue are sticking up. Carefully remove any imperfections with fine sandpaper.

Do this with the frames laid on a flat work surface, and be careful that you do not break anything apart. All of the wing and fuselage surfaces should be taken care of now, for it is necessary to have smooth frames so you can cover them with tissue without having lumps or bumps underneath.

To fasten the tissue paper to the frames, use watered-down Elmer's glue. This can be purchased in almost any hardware store, five-and-ten, or supermarket. The old-timers used a product called Banna oil; if you wish, you can ask your model-store man what he would suggest as the latest cement for fastening model-airplane tissue to balsa frames.

Cut out a piece of tissue large enough to cover one side of the fin, with a bit left over for any necessary adjustment. Now with a brush paint the frame with the glue. You can cover either side. Working from the trailing edge forward, lay the tissue over the frame, stretching it a little at the corners so that it is free of folds or wrinkles. Allow the glue to dry, and be sure that the fin lies flat while the drying process is going on. Be careful not to allow the fin to twist. Pin the fin down, if necessary. When dry, trim off the excess paper with a sharp scissors or an X-acto knife with a new, sharp blade. Wipe the new knife blade clean so that it will be ready for the next trimming job.

Now cover the elevator. This is covered on the top surface only. Put the glue and the tissue covering on in the same way as with the fin. Stretch the paper, pull out any wrinkles or folds, and allow it to dry. Hold it down to a flat surface with pins. Trim the paper off around the wing edges, and be careful not to cut into the balsa wood frame itself.

To cover the main wing is more exacting, although the work is done in the same way. This time, however, you start by putting the paper on from the leading edge, instead of from the trailing edge. The paper goes on from the center rib to the outer rib only. The wing tip covering, from the outer rib to the tip itself, is a separate strip of paper. Do one side at a time.

Put the glue on the wing frame. Cut out a piece of tissue roughly to the size you need, but a bit larger to allow for adjustment. Beginning with the leading edge, lay the tissue on. Then, carefully pulling it back over the top of the ribs, stretch it gently, and just enough to tighten the paper. Now press the paper against the trailing edge, and allow it to dry a bit. Then add the strip of tissue that goes from the outer rib to the wing tip. Set the wing half aside and hold it down with pins until the glue has dried. Then trim off the tissue just as you did with the fin and the elevator. Now cover the other wing half.

We are now ready to glue the halves together and put in the dihedral. To give the wings the proper dihedral, prop up each wing tip with a wooden block or hard-cover book so that the tips are exactly 2⅜″ above your working surface. Glue the wing halves together at the center ribs. Check to make certain that both leading and trailing edges are in line with each other and that the center of the wing is flat on the bench. Allow the wing to dry thoroughly, checking it often to make certain that it does not develop any twists or bends.

When the wing has dried and the dihedral angle is held securely, place the four dihedral wedges beneath the leading and trailing edges. Line the wedges up so that their center line is along the center line of the leading and trailing edges. The points of the wedges should touch. Use enough glue to fasten them securely. Make certain that they are at right angles to the wing and that the bottom surfaces of the wedges are horizontal. You will see how they go by checking the plans.

Now the fuselage is covered. It has tissue paper on all sides except where the elevator fits over the top rear longerons, and of course the forward bulkhead is left without paper at the nose where the motor stick goes into it.

Use the same glue on the longerons of the fuselage as you did for the wings. You need not apply glue to the upright fuselage struts, or to the cross fuselage struts, except where the landing gear is attached. Here you will have to use a small separate sheet of tissue between cross-struts numbers 1 and 2.

It is best to start with the bottom of the fuselage. Put your tissue paper on the fuselage from the tail right up to number 3 cross-strut. The tail skid will not get in the way, for all you do is make a slit in the paper and slip the skid through it. Stretch the paper gently until it is tight and wrinkle-free. Add a small piece up to the nose. It may be a bit hard to get the tissue tight and smooth between the landing gear struts, but if you work slowly and with patience it can be done. Allow all the glue to dry before you attempt to cover the top of the fuselage.

Cover the fuselage top from the rear bulkhead forward. Make certain that the tissue here, also, is free from wrinkles. And make certain that you don't pull the fuselage out of line while you are stretching the tissue over the frame. When both top and bottom sections have dried, trim the tissue away with your knife, being very careful not to take off any of the balsa wood.

The top and bottom trimming should be done so that there is no excess left on the edges that will get in the way of the side covering. If you are not careful here, the sides will have a series of little lumps and you will not have a properly covered fuselage.

Cover each side of the fuselage separately. Allow each side to dry before doing the other. The fuselage sides are coverd from tail to nose. Get the covering smooth and wrinkle-free, and you will have a fine-looking piece of work. Remember, do not twist the fuselage out of line while covering it. Check frequently to make sure of this.

All you have to do after the fuselage has been covered and the tissue trimmed clean is to put the tail assembly in place. First glue the elevator to the rear of the fuselage. It fits against the rear bulkhead and on top of the exposed rear longerons. Be sure that the elevator is at right angles to the fuselage when you look at it from the front or rear, and that it is also square to the center line of the fuselage looking at it from the top. A small metal square will help you check the alignment of your model.

The fin is glued to the center line of the elevator and must line up with the center line of the fuselage; that is, it must be on a straight line, front to back. If the fin does not stick in place properly, cut away some of the tissue at the elevator's leading and trailing edges where they touch and apply more glue. Hold the tail assembly in position with small pins until dry. Be careful when you place and remove the pins that you do not crack the wood.

The main wing, which goes on top of the fuselage, usually over numbers 2, 3, and 4 cross-struts, can be held in place with a rubber band carefully stretched over the wing and about the fuselage. The rubber band (and it should be a large one) is first passed through the struts of the landing gear. Then both ends are drawn up alongside the fuselage, over the wing, and finally down the fuselage sides. A wire or wood dowel $\frac{1}{16}''$ in diameter is inserted through the looped ends below the fuselage at number 4 bottom cross-strut.

The rubber band used must be tight enough to hold the wing in position, *without putting any strain on either fuselage or wing*. It also must allow the wing to be moved forward or back for proper flying adjustment.

Now test the flying qualities of the model. Insert the motor stick, but do not wind up the rubber motor. Do your testing in the same way as you did with the R.O.G. Find a place free of obstructions for the test flight. Place the wheels on the ground, raise the tail to make your model level, and give it a gentle push forward. If the plane hops off the ground gently and comes to an easy landing, then the model is about right. You can then test it from arm height by gently throwing it forward. But this should be done only over tall grass or over some place where the model will not be damaged if it dives steeply. If the model glides gently downward, then you are ready for powered flights. If it noses down, move the wing forward until a gentle glide is obtained. The same is true for ground launching. If the model does not hop off and land easily, adjust the main wing, either forward or to the rear, until it does. When hand launching is tried, you will be able to make any necessary further adjustments.

Now go through the same process: first ground launching and then hand launching, but this time remove the motor stick and wind the motor, turning the propeller to the right when facing it until about half a row of knots forms in the rubber. Replace in the fuselage.

Hold the propeller tip and the tip of the fin, when ground launching. Let the propeller go for an instant and give the plane a gentle push forward. It should climb easily and, when the propeller winds out, glide to a good landing.

You may have to insert a piece of balsa wood between the rear of the fuselage and the trailing edge of the elevator in order to help obtain the right glide angle, even though you have moved the main wing. You will have to slip your X-acto knife between the elevator and slice away some of the glue in order to insert the piece. This may be absolutely necessary in order to get the plane to fly well. A $\frac{1}{8}''$ by $\frac{1}{16}''$ by $2''$ piece of wood should do the trick. This raises the rear of the elevator and causes the nose to rise.

Adjustment for really good flights may take a bit of time, but it is worth it in the end. Once the model is all set, fine, long flight can be made with it. After a while you will learn how many times to wind the propeller for different flights, how to make the plane climb steeply, and how to make long glides to a good landing. But be careful that you do not overwind the rubber. One and a half rows of knots should be enough. You may also find that two instead of three lengths of rubber are enough for the kind of flight you want; then, two rows of knots can be attempted. Always wind the rubber motor with the stick out of the airplane. This way, it will not be damaged if the rubber snaps. Fly it only on calm days. Windy days will send your model down to the best crack-up you ever saw!

Remember to take your time building the Fuselage Flying Model, and adjusting it for good flights. Take care and use patience, and you will be rewarded with many hours of great model-airplane flying.

Chapter 7

How to Build a Cardboard Scale Airplane Model

It is a good idea now to make your experience work for you in a slightly different direction, that of scale model making. Do not suppose that scale models cannot be just as much fun to build as action models, for they can! Many builders would rather construct a detailed model that does not fly because it gives them the chance to make something almost like the real thing.

The plans are in two sections for the Waco 10 airplane. First is the three-view plan, which shows you how the real airplane looks from the side, the top and the front, and also what the model will look like when completed. You will refer to it often, while making the model, because these views will be your guide during assembly.

The second section of the plans includes the patterns that you will trace on cardboard, then cut out and glue together to form the fuselage and the wings. The landing gear, the wing struts and the engine are made of wood.

Some model makers like to make their models solid—of balsa or pine wood. For this they also use a three-view plan almost exactly like the one shown in this chapter. Therefore, if you like and think you can carve out a model from solid wood, you can try to make one, using the three-view drawings as your guide. Since we are concerned

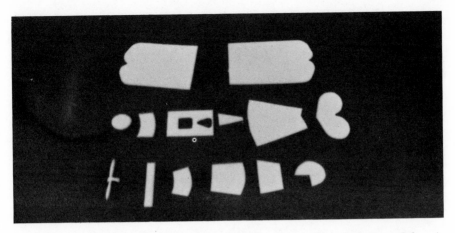

The fuselage and wing patterns for the Waco 10 cardboard plane model.
(*Kirt Miska*)

at this time with making a cardboard model, we shall concentrate on it and leave you to your own devices, with respect to carving a wooden model.

The most important thing in cardboard model making is to make certain that all bends, folds, and creases are made *with the grain of the cardboard*. This can be made clearer to you if you take a piece of scrap material and try it yourself. You will discover that when you bend or curve with the grain of the cardboard, it will readily form to the shape you want; but, when bent or curved against the grain, it will crack and become useless.

Cardboard models can be made to be just as accurate as most solid wood scale models. They are durable, long-lasting, and very inexpensive to build.

The choice of cardboard is, of course, up to the maker. Several types of cardboard can be used, but others cannot. You cannot use very hard, thick, or stiff cardboard, nor can you use the corrugated kind—the type cartons are made of.

About the best material for this particular model is the type of cardboard that comes with laundered shirts. If you don't have any, your art store has other stock, such as show card or "railroad board." If you must purchase cardboard, get thin stock—material that will bend easily. A sheet that will last for a dozen models should cost you about thirty-five cents.

You can use the same quick-drying glue as you did for your flying models, and of course your X-acto knife and other tools will be of service here as well. Just make sure that your scissors are sharp and that you keep them and your fingers free from glue at all times when assembling the Waco 10. Glue on the scissors tears the parts when you

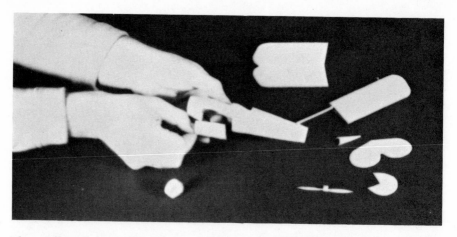

The cardboard parts of the Waco 10 plane—wings, tail assembly, headrest, propeller and engine base. The piece shown being inserted is the lower part of the fuselage above the lower wing. (*Kirt Miska*)

are cutting them out and glue on the fingers not only tears away some of the cardboard where you place your fingers but also leaves smears and rough, uneven marks that cannot be removed either with sandpaper or with anything else. Be very careful.

The top wing for the Waco 10 model is 10½″ long. The model itself is 8″ long from the front of the standard steel propeller to the back of the rudder. By these measurements, you can see that you will have a nice-sized model—one that will fit readily on almost any shelf in your room.

Have the patterns all brought up to the measurements given on the plans, and do not use guesswork. If you match one measurement, then all the other measurements will automatically enlarge to the correct size when plans are photo-enlarged. However, since several different model makers will make their models of various kinds of cardboard, some allowance has been made for this in the original drawings. You may find, therefore, that adjustments in size may have to be made in your individual case.

The patterns are the first thing to study. You will see that there is a pattern for the rear of the fuselage. This is numbered 1. The top sections of the fuselage are numbered 2 and 3. The bottom sections of the fuselage are numbered 4, 5, and 6. The circular piece A is made to insert into the pieces marked 3 and 6, and piece C is to be wrapped about the disk marked B. The headrest goes on the fuselage behind the rear cockpit atop number 2. The standard steel type propeller, of course, goes at the nose.

There are only four patterns given for the flying surfaces. The main or top wing is made in one piece even though the pattern is given in half-section. However, the bottom wing is actually made in separate halves.

The rudder, fin and elevator are made from single pieces of cardboard and are not folded over, as are the main and lower wings.

All strutwork, for the wings as well as for the landing gear, is made of hard balsa wood, or of pine or bass wood. The wheels may be made up, but for this particular model, being scale, it is better to purchase them. They are obtainable with rubber tires and the correct pair will add a great deal to the appearance of your model. The diameter of the wheels is $\frac{7}{8}''$. Wheels should never be made larger than this. They must have narrow tires to be in scale.

The Wright "J" 2 Whirlwind radial engine has nine cylinders, air-cooled. The real engine was rated at 200 horsepower. Since building the model of the engine may be found to be a tricky job for most modelers at this stage, it is suggested that one from a plastic airplane kit be used, or that one be purchased. However, later on in this chapter a description for constructing a Whirlwind engine for this model will be outlined. The engine's diameter should be about $1\frac{1}{2}''$.

Now that you have a general idea of the parts and where they go, begin by cutting out fuselage section number 1. This may look confusing at first, but as you gently curve it (do not attempt to fold or bend this section), and as the edges meet where the arrows are, you will see it take shape. The seam where the arrows meet comes on the side about $\frac{5}{8}''$ down from the top of the section at its front, and $\frac{1}{4}''$ down at the back. Mark where the bottom line goes, for, if you do not, you will never know which end is up.

The two edges marked with the arrows are glued together at the back as well. The seam can be held in position with cellophane tape placed on the inside and with a paper clip at the back; or rubber bands can hold it until the glue has dried.

Next cut out pattern number 2. Remember to cut out the two cockpit openings now; it cannot be done later. Curve the section to conform with the curve of the front top half of number 1 section; and if the glue on number 1 has dried and it holds its oval shape, you can glue the number 2 cockpit section to it. It should come just about halfway down on each side.

Number 4 section is cut out next, and is curved until it fits below the rear of the cockpit section and against the rear section. Then it should be glued in place. From here on you may have to trim off a bit, now and again, in order to make the pieces match. This is due, usually, to the different kinds of cardboard used. It is doubtful that anyone will use exactly the same kind of cardboard as that from which the original model was made.

Section number 5 should be cut out next. It, too, is curved and glued in place. Trim it to fit if necessary. Do not forget to mark the center lines so that you can line up all the fuselage sections accurately. If a part does not fit, even after you have trimmed it, or because you forgot to line the pattern up with the grain of the cardboard, make it over. It is a simple task to make a new piece, so do not take a chance and spoil the model with a part that does not fit properly.

Now cut out section number 3. Curve it to fit against the front of the cockpit section. The rear edges should line up with the bottom of the cockpit piece. Glue it in place.

After section number 3 has dried in position, cut out the remaining piece, number 6. This is the lower front part of the fuselage, and gives it its final shape. Fit it below section number 3 and to number 5.

All sections may be held together with rubber bands. But make certain that the rubber bands hold the pieces securely in place without adding stress to them. If the rubber bands are too tight, they will simply buckle the fuselage. Cellophane tape may be used inside the seams wherever you want it. It does not have to be removed after the glue has dried, for it will not be seen.

The disks marked A and B can be cut out now. It is wise to make two of each and glue them together for strength, crossing the grain of the cardboard so that they do not bend when they are put in position.

The disk marked A goes inside fuselage sections numbers 3 and 6. Insert it so that the disk is flush with the front of these sections. Make certain that it is square (straight up and down and across). Glue it in place and, when it has dried securely, trim off any excess cardboard from sections 3 and 6. A word about this: the front ends of sections 3 and 6 may not come out absolutely evenly, so do not attempt

Showing model ready to have struts made and the top wing put in place.
(*Kirt Miska*)

68

Details of landing gear struts and N struts in the cardboard Waco 10 plane.
(*Kirt Miska*)

to line up disk A with them; instead, trim off and align the front of sections 3 and 6 with the disk.

While this is drying you can make up the motor base, which consists of parts C and disk B. However, if you have purchased a radial model engine in plastic, you do not need parts C or B. Cement the engine to disk A as soon as the glue has dried and you have finished trimming the edges, as mentioned above. Remember that you must position the engine so that its center line goes through the center of disk A. The hole that takes the propeller is the engine's center. Also make certain that one cylinder is placed exactly on top and two are positioned at the bottom.

If you build the engine, construct it of balsa wood. Make nine cylinders from either a 9″ length of balsa dowel, ¼″ in diameter, or round a 9″ length of ¼″-square balsa wood with sandpaper. Each cylinder should be ³⁄₁₆″ to ¼″ high.

Another way to make the nine engine cylinders is with a paper punch. Punch many ¼″ disks out of stiff paper, cardboard, ¹⁄₆₄″-thick balsa wood, or thin aluminum. In between each disk insert another disk a bit smaller—say, ³⁄₁₆″ in diameter—until you have built up each cylinder to the height of ³⁄₁₆″ to ¼″. You have leeway because of building material differences.

Assume that the motor base, parts B and C, has been made by simply wrapping C around disk B so that one edge of piece C is flush with the disk. If there is any extra length and you see that you have an overlapping joint where the edges of the cardboard strip C should come together, trim it off carefully until the ends butt exactly, then glue it all together.

When the motor base is complete and the glue dry, face the disk forward and put glue around the edge of piece C. Glue it against disk A. Make certain that you line it up so that you can run a long pin through the exact center of each.

After the motor base has dried in position, you can begin to place in position the nine cylinders that you have made. Put one cylinder at the top center, and two at the bottom, then space the rest evenly at either side.

To the front of each cylinder glue two lengths of wire, $\frac{3}{16}''$ long, spacing them so that each wire just about runs up and down the width of the cylinder at the front. These are the pushrods for the engine valves. Then on top of each cylinder place two bits of wood $\frac{1}{16}''$ square and $\frac{3}{16}''$ long. Space them $\frac{1}{16}''$ in from the outer edge of the cylinder. These represent the covers for the overhead-valve activating parts. Simply glue them in place. The engine color is black.

Save the propeller and the headrest for later on. They can be cut out now, though, and put aside until the model is about completed. Remember to roll the center part of the propeller so that it forms a solid cylindrical hub. Use a pin to fasten it to the engine when you are ready.

The lower wing is made now. Cut out your patterns, right and left. Keep the cardboard grain running the long way. Mark out the ailerons in pencil so that you will know where they are located. Very carefully fold each wing-half together so that the trailing edges and the wing tips come together exactly. Now very gently crease the leading edge with your fingers. Place the wing halves on your working board when you do this so that you do not wrap the wing. When you're certain that each lower wing-half matches properly, you can glue the edges together. Do not glue the inner edge that touches the fuselage. You can hold the trailing edges and the wing tips together by weighing them down until the glue has dried. You will find that you now have two quite strong wings with a built-in aerofoil. Check the tips to see that they are in a straight line where they have been glued together. Also check that the lower wing-halves lie flat and even on your work board. Correct any defects either by making new wing halves or by taking them apart and re-gluing.

In order to hold the lower wing to the fuselage, a piece of wood (hard balsa or pine, 5″ long and measuring $\frac{3}{16}''$ by $\frac{5}{16}''$) is used as a spar.

Insert this spar into each half of the wing, about $\frac{3}{8}''$ back from the leading edge, and then place the lower wings against the fuselage bottom. The leading edge should come about $\frac{3}{4}''$ back from where disk A is. With the lower wings spread apart so that the wing measures $9\frac{3}{4}''$ from tip to tip, mark the place where the spar touches the bottom of the fuselage. Check to see that the leading edge is straight.

Ready for paint, wires and cockpit windshield. (*Kirt Miska*)

If the bottom of the wing and the bottom of the fuselage line up, the wing is in its proper position. You may have to cut a slot in the fuselage bottom to take the spar in order to bring the lower wing up to its correct position. Use your three-view plan to find the exact placement.

Next glue in place the inner edges of the wing-halves and the spar, where they touch the fuselage. See that each half is exactly in line with the other and square to the fuselage. By pressing up at the tips you can get a dihedral of $\frac{1}{8}''$ on each side. Hold this dihedral in place with books just as you did with your flying models. Allow the wings to dry to the fuselage thoroughly. Fill in the space between the wing-half and the fuselage, bottom and sides, with model putty. With sandpaper, streamline the wing to the fuselage after the putty has dried overnight. Be careful not to rough up the cardboard when you sandpaper.

The top wing is shown in half section. However, you must double the pattern over so that the wing is cut out in one complete piece $10\frac{1}{2}''$ long.

Mark the ailerons with pencil, and carefully fold over the upper wing until the trailing edges and the wing tips touch. Crease the leading edge, just as you did with the lower wing. See that the edges to be glued together meet exactly, and that the wing will be without wrappage when glued together.

Before you put the glue in place, you can add strength, if you wish, by placing in the wing $\frac{3}{8}''$ back from the leading edge a $9''$-long piece of hard balsa wood measuring $\frac{3}{16}''$ by $\frac{5}{16}''$. Glue it in place and let the glue dry before joining together the trailing edges and the tips. The upper wing does not have a dihedral angle, so you can hold the wing down on a flat surface until the edges have dried together.

Check the wing tips and the trailing edge once more to make

certain that the wing is in line and without twists. Put it aside for the moment and make the six wing struts. Two on each side act as the wing spars, and one on each side connects the upper and lower wing ailerons. The two center struts are N-shaped and are made of three pieces of hard balsa wood, just as you see on the plans. Measurements for the wood and the size of the struts are indicated. Note that the right-side center strut is placed in position as an N turned backward.

Cut each outboard strut to length and then carefully streamline them by rounding the front and making the back come almost to a point. Be careful when using sandpaper here that you don't break your struts, or you will have nothing left.

When the six outboard struts are complete, make your center struts, the two Ns. Each N is made of three pieces. Streamline each piece. Place the front and rear leg of the N on your working board and hold in place with pins. Then insert the cross-leg of the N between them, glue together, and let dry thoroughly. Use a piece of waxed paper between the wood struts and your work board to keep them from sticking to the board. Note that there is a slant to the front and rear legs of the N. You might draw out the struts on a piece of paper and lay the wood over it if you want a more accurate set of inboard struts.

When all the struts are finished, and the excess glue, if any, has been carefully sandpapered away, you can put the struts in position. Begin with the two N inboard struts. They are placed at the sides near the top of the fuselage with the rear bottom of the N just about in line with the front of the forward cockpit opening, as you will see by looking at the side view of the three-view plan. The rear leg of the N touches the fuselage side about ¼″ down from the top of the fuselage and the forward leg is in horizontal line with it.

You will see, on the front view of the three-view plan, that the inboard, or center, struts are spread apart at the top. The distance between the struts here is about 1¾″. You may have to adjust this after the outboard struts are in place. The best thing to do now is to fix them to the fuselage with small pins inserted through the bottom of the struts.

Now put the outboard struts in position; use only two struts on each side, the aileron strut coming later. Again referring to the three-view plan, you can see that the outboard struts tilt toward the wing tips at the top, ⅛″ farther from the fuselage than the bottom. The bottom of the struts should be placed about 2¾″ out from the fuselage.

Another thing to observe is that the struts stagger forward; that is, they tilt frontward. So line up the leading edge of the top wing so that the inboard N struts touch the top wing ⅛″ in from the leading edge. Glue the outboard struts to the bottom wing. The front strut goes ⅛″ back from the leading edge and the rear strut ¹³⁄₁₆″ back of it. Hold them in place with very small pins carefully pushed through the wood so that the strut does not break, and let them tilt forward and outward at the top. Now run small pins the same way through the top of the N struts into the top wing, deeply enough to hold the wing in position with the Ns spread apart enough to allow the wing to touch the top of the outboard struts. As explained before, the inboard struts marked N have to be spread apart about 1¾″, but you may have to use more or less than that in order to have all the struts touch the top wing at once. Once they do, glue the wing to the struts with enough glue to hold them securely in position.

Check the position of the top wing and make certain that when you look down on it, it is square to the fuselage, and that the leading and trailing edges of both wings are along the same line (but with, of course, the top wing farther forward). If you look carefully at the three-view plan again, you will know exactly how the wings are placed and how the struts go. Allow the glue to dry, and then gently and with a twisting motion, using a flat-nosed pliers, remove the pins. Insert and glue the aileron struts about ⁵⁄₁₆″ behind the outboard struts. They line up exactly with them.

The landing gear comes next. It is made of six struts. Four are V-shaped and two are long, plain struts, which on the real craft act as shock absorbers. Using the three-view plan, you can see that the four struts that make the V come together at the bottom center of the fuselage, and that the shock struts touch the V only where the axle and the wheels are fastened.

The best way to position the struts is to line up the bottom of

This side view of the Waco 10 shows how the cardboard pieces are fitted together.
(*Kirt Miska*)

the V with the bottom of the N inboard wing struts, as shown on the three-view plan. Carefully lay the model on the top wing, so that the bottom of the fuselage faces upward. Put glue on the tips of the landing gear struts and place them in position along the center of the bottom of the fuselage. Hold them in place with pins in the same manner as you did with the wing struts. Now before the glue has a chance to dry, glue the shock struts in place. Let them come down about ⅛″ below the front leg of the N wing strut, on either side. Glue and pin them in position. When you glue the shock struts to the V strut, the V strut will part automatically and give you the right spread.

After the glue has thoroughly dried, put the wheels on. If you want to make them, simply cut out several cardboard disks about ⅞″ in diameter and glue them together until they are as near to ⅛″ thick as you can get. Sandpaper the edges after the disks have dried together until the edges are smooth, then round the edges so that the center of the "tire" is higher than the rim. Paint the tire on the wheel with flat black model paint. The tire is ⅛″ wide along the side of the wheel. Paint the tire on both front and back of each wheel. Allow the paint to dry, then, with a small pin run through the center of each wheel, push the pin through the shock strut and the bottom of the V strut. Fasten the pin in place with glue. Note that the wheels tilt outward a little at the top. Clip off any of the pin that sticks out. Be careful here that you do not crack or bend anything while clipping off the pin. Use a good, sharp wire side-cutter.

Now you can set the plane on its wheels. See that it sits evenly and that the wheels are in exactly the same position on each side. Next insert a piece of piano wire, ¹⁄₃₂″ in diameter and about ¾″ long, into the tail of the fuselage so that half of it sticks out. It should slant sharply backward. Glue it securely in place. This is your tail skid, and with it installed, the landing gear of the Waco 10 model is complete.

You now have only the tail assembly to cut out and glue onto the fuselage. So trace out the elevator on to your cardboard, and then the rudder and fin, which are made in a single unit in this case.

There is a choice here. To give you a stronger assembly and one that can be streamlined, you can glue together two cardboard cut-outs of the elevator and of the rudder. Or just use single pieces of cardboard.

If you glue two pieces together, round the leading edges with fine sandpaper when the glue has dried and lightly taper the trailing edges, just as you did with the flying models. If the cardboard appears a bit rough after it is sandpapered, then, with your finger, rub a little glue over the roughness until it smooths out.

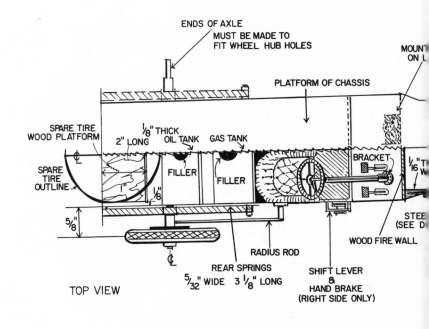

ENDS OF AXLE
MUST BE MADE TO
FIT WHEEL HUB HOLES

PLATFORM OF CHASSIS

MOUNT
ON L

SPARE TIRE
WOOD PLATFORM

1/8" THICK
2" LONG   OIL TANK   GAS TANK

BRACKET

1/16" TH
W

SPARE
TIRE
OUTLINE

FILLER   FILLER

1/8"   1"

STEE
(SEE D

5/8"

WOOD FIRE WALL

RADIUS ROD

REAR SPRINGS
5/32" WIDE   3 1/8" LONG

SHIFT LEVER
&
HAND BRAKE
(RIGHT SIDE ONLY)

TOP VIEW

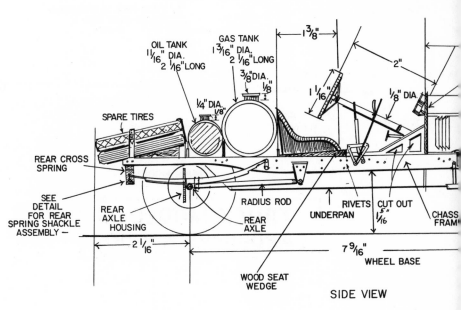

OIL TANK
11/16" DIA.
2 1/16" LONG

GAS TANK
1 3/16" DIA.
2 1/16" LONG

3/8" DIA.
1/8"

1 3/8"

2"

1 1/16"

1/8" DIA.

1/4" DIA.
1/8"

SPARE TIRES

REAR CROSS
SPRING

RADIUS ROD

RIVETS   CUT OUT
5"
1/16

CHASS
FRAM

SEE
DETAIL
FOR REAR
SPRING SHACKLE
ASSEMBLY —

REAR
AXLE
HOUSING

REAR
AXLE

UNDERPAN

2 1/16"

7 9/16"

WHEEL BASE

WOOD SEAT
WEDGE

SIDE VIEW

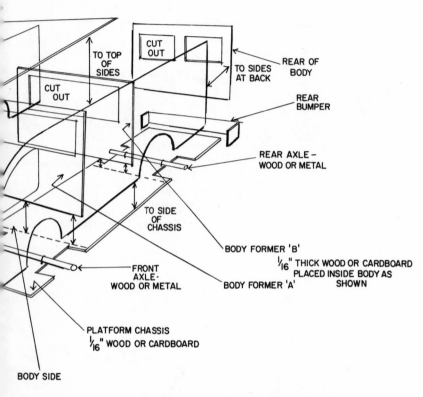

CUT OUT

TO TOP OF SIDES

REAR OF BODY

TO SIDES AT BACK

CUT OUT

REAR BUMPER

REAR AXLE – WOOD OR METAL

TO SIDE OF CHASSIS

BODY FORMER 'B'

$\frac{1}{16}$" THICK WOOD OR CARDBOARD PLACED INSIDE BODY AS SHOWN

BODY FORMER 'A'

FRONT AXLE - WOOD OR METAL

PLATFORM CHASSIS $\frac{1}{16}$" WOOD OR CARDBOARD

BODY SIDE

ASSEMBLY OF TRUCK MODEL

TRUCK MODEL OF CARDBOARD & WOOD

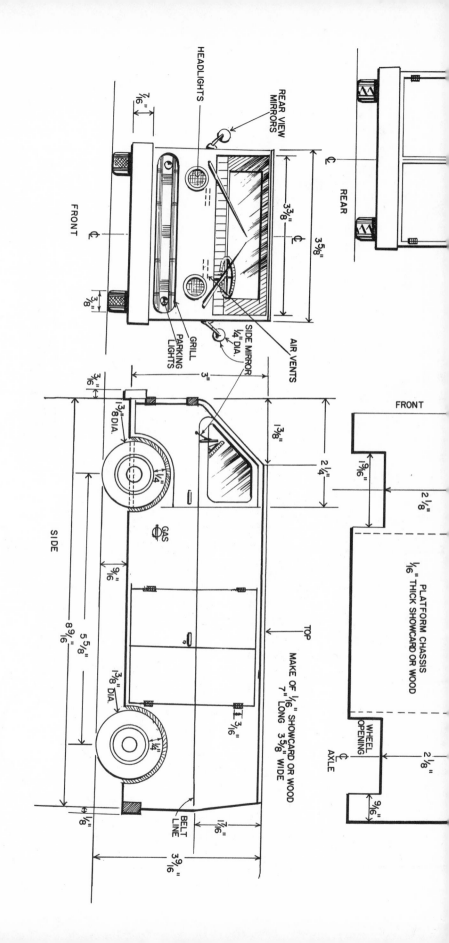

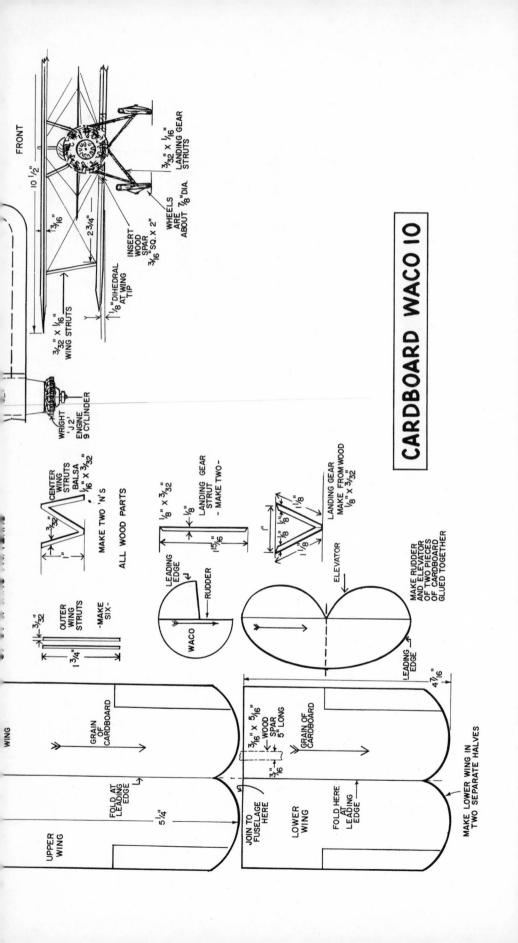

CARDBOARD WACO 10

FRONT

10 1/2"

3/16"

2 3/4"

1/8" DIHEDRAL AT WING TIP

3/32" x 1/16" WING STRUTS

INSERT WOOD SPAR 3/16" SQ. x 2"

3/32" x 1/16" LANDING GEAR STRUTS

WHEELS ARE ABOUT 7/8" DIA.

WRIGHT 'J2' ENGINE 9 CYLINDER

CENTER WING STRUTS BALSA 1/16" x 3/32"

3/32"

1"

MAKE TWO 'N'S

ALL WOOD PARTS

3/32"

OUTER WING STRUTS -MAKE SIX-

1 3/4"

1/8" x 3/32"

1/8"

LANDING GEAR STRUT - MAKE TWO -

1 15/16"

LEADING EDGE

RUDDER

WACO

1/8"

1/8"

1"

1/8"

1 1/8"

LANDING GEAR MAKE FROM WOOD 1/8" x 3/32"

ELEVATOR

LEADING EDGE

4 7/16"

MAKE RUDDER AND ELEVATOR OF TWO PIECES OF CARDBOARD GLUED TOGETHER

WING

GRAIN OF CARDBOARD

UPPER WING

FOLD AT LEADING EDGE

5 1/4"

JOIN TO FUSELAGE HERE

3/16" x 5/16" WOOD SPAR 5" LONG

3/16"

GRAIN OF CARDBOARD

LOWER WING

FOLD HERE AT LEADING EDGE

MAKE LOWER WING IN TWO SEPARATE HALVES

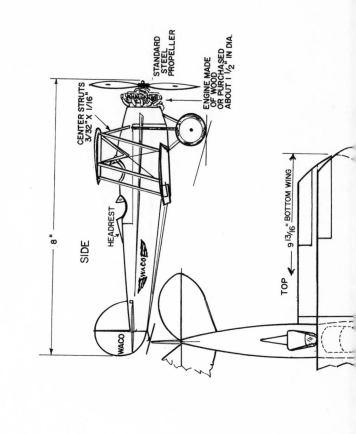

STANDARD
STEEL
PROPELLER

ENGINE MADE
OF WOOD
OR PURCHASED
ABOUT 1 1/2" IN DIA.

CENTER STRUTS
3/32" x 1/16"

8"

HEADREST

WACO

WACO

SIDE

TOP

9 13/16" BOTTOM WING

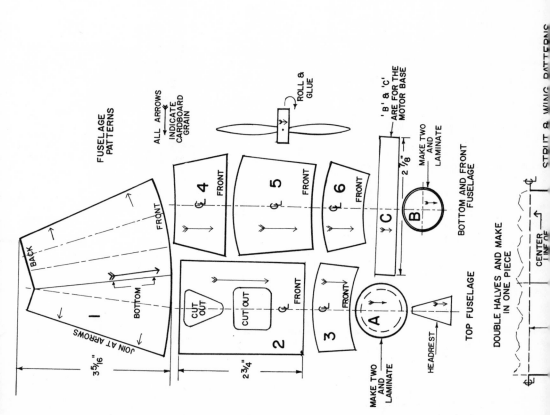

FUSELAGE
PATTERNS

ALL ARROWS
INDICATE
CARDBOARD
GRAIN

ROLL &
GLUE

FRONT

BACK

BOTTOM

1

3 5/16"

JOIN AT ARROWS

CUT
OUT

CUT OUT

FRONT

2

2 3/4"

MAKE TWO
AND LAMINATE

FRONT

3

HEADREST

FRONT

4

FRONT

5

FRONT

6

A

B

C

'B' & 'C'
ARE FOR THE
MOTOR BASE

2 7/8"

MAKE TWO
AND LAMINATE

BOTTOM AND FRONT
FUSELAGE

TOP FUSELAGE

DOUBLE HALVES AND MAKE
IN ONE PIECE

CENTER
LINE OF

STRUT & WING PATTERNS

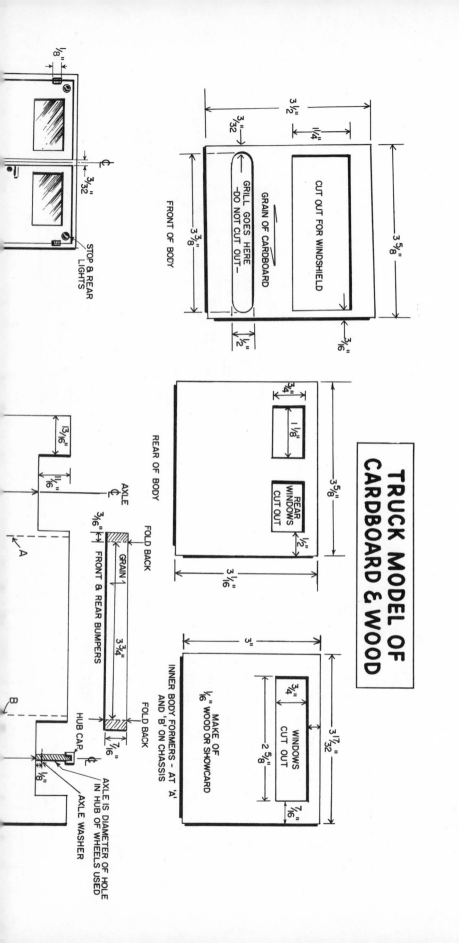

TRUCK MODEL OF CARDBOARD & WOOD

FRONT OF BODY

CUT OUT FOR WINDSHIELD

GRILL GOES HERE
—DO NOT CUT OUT—

GRAIN OF CARDBOARD

3 1/2"

1/4"

3/32"

3 5/8"

3 3/8"

3/16"

1/2"

STOP & REAR LIGHTS

1/8"

3/32"

REAR OF BODY

REAR WINDOWS CUT OUT

3/4"

1/8"

1/2"

3 5/8"

3 1/16"

13/16"

1 1/16"

AXLE ℄

FOLD BACK

3/16"

GRAIN

FRONT & REAR BUMPERS

3 3/4"

FOLD BACK

7/16"

A

B

HUB CAP

℄

1/8"

AXLE WASHER

AXLE IS DIAMETER OF HOLE IN HUB OF WHEELS USED

INNER BODY FORMERS – AT 'A'
AND 'B' ON CHASSIS

MAKE OF 1/16" WOOD OR SHOWCARD

WINDOWS CUT OUT

3/4"

2 5/8"

7/16"

3"

3 17/32"

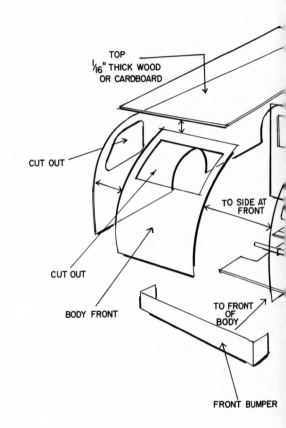

TOP
$\frac{1}{16}$" THICK WOOD
OR CARDBOARD

CUT OUT

TO SIDE AT
FRONT

CUT OUT

BODY FRONT

TO FRONT
OF
BODY

FRONT BUMPER

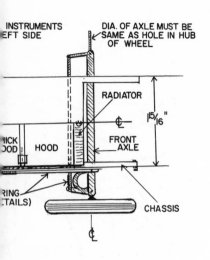

INSTRUMENTS
LEFT SIDE

DIA. OF AXLE MUST BE
SAME AS HOLE IN HUB
OF WHEEL

RADIATOR

THICK
WOOD   HOOD

FRONT
AXLE

1 5/16"

SPRING
(DETAILS)

CHASSIS

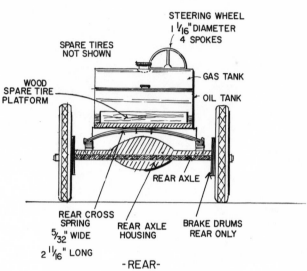

SPARE TIRES
NOT SHOWN

STEERING WHEEL
1 1/16" DIAMETER
4 SPOKES

WOOD
SPARE TIRE
PLATFORM

GAS TANK

OIL TANK

REAR AXLE

REAR CROSS
SPRING
5/32" WIDE

2 11/16" LONG

REAR AXLE
HOUSING

BRAKE DRUMS
REAR ONLY

- REAR -

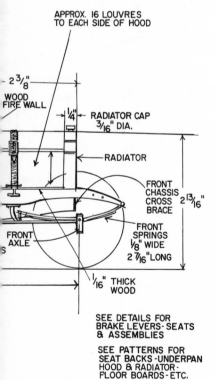

APPROX. 16 LOUVRES
TO EACH SIDE OF HOOD

- 2 3/8"
WOOD
FIRE WALL

1/4"

RADIATOR CAP
3/16" DIA.

RADIATOR

FRONT
CHASSIS
CROSS
BRACE

2 13/16"

FRONT
SPRINGS
1/8" WIDE
2 7/16" LONG

FRONT
AXLE

1/16" THICK
WOOD

SEE DETAILS FOR
BRAKE LEVERS - SEATS
& ASSEMBLIES

SEE PATTERNS FOR
SEAT BACKS - UNDERPAN
HOOD & RADIATOR -
FLOOR BOARDS - ETC.

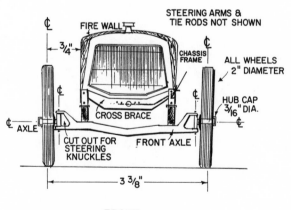

STEERING ARMS &
TIE RODS NOT SHOWN

FIRE WALL

3/4"

CHASSIS
FRAME

ALL WHEELS
2" DIAMETER

CROSS BRACE

HUB CAP
3/16" DIA.

AXLE

CUT OUT FOR
STEERING
KNUCKLES

FRONT AXLE

3 3/8"

- FRONT -

1910 RACING CAR

For remainder of Racing Car plans,
see chapter 9.

You can still round all the edges of the tail assembly even if you use single pieces, but put glue on the sandpapered edges to keep them smooth.

When the elevator and the rudder are completed, glue the elevator in position on the top of the fuselage. Make certain that it is square and in line when you look at it from the top, the front and the back. It should line up as shown on the three-view plan. Allow the glue to dry and then attach the rudder, which must stand exactly upright and be in line, front to back, with the center line of the fuselage. Both elevator and rudder can be held in position either by propping up with wooden blocks or by using small pins carefully inserted into the cardboard.

After the glue has dried, and if you used pins, remove them with a twisting motion. Be careful not to damage any parts. The assembly of the Waco 10 is finished. You can paint it now.

The colors for the model can be of the builder's choice. However, one of the original color combinations is all silver, with deep blue around the engine, almost back to the landing gear shock strut, and at the top of the fuselage around the cockpit, including the headrest. The name WACO appears on either side of the rudder, just above the elevator, and on the fuselage sides, just ahead of the elevator. Deep blue can be painted on the top of the lower wing in a strip 1″ wide where it meets the fuselage. The propeller, wheel centers, and tail skid are painted aluminum.

The engine is flat black. If you wish, you may make a spinner for the propeller, or you may purchase one. This is either silver or deep blue. Deep blue can also be used for the landing gear struts.

The "wire" bracing, made of thin thread, goes between the wings. Loop it about the struts where they touch the wing and glue it. Be very careful that you do not pull the struts away from the wing, and that you not allow the glue to run all over your newly painted surfaces. Use Elmer's glue for this work.

The "wiring" forms an X from the struts to the fuselage front and back, and also another X between the outboard wing struts. Trim off any excess wiring with your X-acto knife. Last of all, install the propeller, using a long pin to hold it in place. It need not be made to turn; so if you wish, a drop of glue can be added to hold it in any position you desire. Your model of the Waco 10 is now completed.

Chapter 8

The Panel Truck Model

A modern truck was chosen for our first automotive model because it is basically easy to construct.

The chassis of our truck is simply a flat board with cutouts made for the four wheels. The body is very like a square box and consists of only seven cardboard parts. Possibly the only units you may have to purchase are the four wheels and the steering wheel. However, if you wish, you can make these things yourself.

First of all, as it is advised for all the models, look at the plans. Notice the details of the truck. Acquaint yourself with the method of construction as shown to you in the exploded view and the other drawings. Then read the text thoroughly. Try to build the model in your mind before you actually start work. Also think out beforehand what tools the model will require for its construction and have them ready.

You can also think about the printing that will go on the truck body sides and whether or not you want to use a transparent plastic for the windows; also about putting a seat inside and adding details of your own. Custom details are permissible, most trucks being fitted out in one way or another to suit their owners. Read the instructions and study the plans. Then begin the truck model.

Obtain a piece of wood 8%₁₆″ long, 3½″ wide and ³⁄₃₂″ or ⅛″ thick. This is for the platform or chassis. Cut out the chassis as shown on the plans.

Make certain that all the edges of the platform are square and that the wood used is free from warps or twists. Use your flat X-acto sandpaper block and fine sandpaper to finish off the platform. Sandpaper the edges as well as the top and bottom. Try not to round the corners of the wheel hollows. Make sure that they are 1%₁₆″ wide and 1¹⁄₁₆″ deep. The distance from the front of the chassis to the front wheel wells is ¹³⁄₁₆″ while the distance to the rear wheel wells is %₁₆″. Remember this difference in measurements or you might put the front to the back and nothing will fit.

The diameter of the axles will depend on the kind of wheels you will use and the size of their hub center where the axle goes through. If you use a wheel with a ¼″ opening, the axle will naturally have to have a diameter of ¼″. If the wheel hub has an opening of ⅛″, the axle must be ⅛″ in diameter.

Let us assume that your wheels will have a ⅛″ hub opening. You will then need two ⅛″-diameter axles, one for the front and one for the rear. Both can be of wood dowel but brass tubing or rod may also be used. Front and rear axles are 3½″ long. They are fastened to the platform with glue and two pins bent to a U shape, after you cut off the head. The U-shaped pins are placed over the axle about ¼″ in from the wheel hollows. After the axles are in place and have some glue on them, hammer the U-shaped pins into the platform, as shown on the plans. Make certain that the axles extend the same distance on each side from the center line of the platform.

The wheels, whether purchased or made, should be 1⅜″, or as close as you can get to that, in diameter. They should be about ⅜″ wide. Tire height, measuring from the wheel to the top of the tread, should be ¼″. If nothing else can be found, you may be able to use model-airplane wheels that answer your need. However, these usually have extremely small hub openings. If you have to use this kind of wheel, wire to fit the diameter of the wheel hub will have to be used in place of the larger diameter wood or brass axles.

Looking at the top view of the chassis platform, you will note that a washer is placed on each axle. These may be brass or aluminum and are ⅜″ in diameter. The center should be of the same diameter as the axle you use. You might, however, have to enlarge the washer centers to fit your particular axle. These washers are glued in place ⅛″ out from the inside of the wheel well, as shown. They stop the wheels from touching the chassis. Place one on each axle side— four in all. Make certain that they are glued securely.

Now, if you have a wheel that for some reason is of a different

This picture of a real truck of the type for which working plans are included in this book will be helpful as you build the cardboard model.

width from the ⅜″ wheel mentioned, you will, naturally, have to change the placement of the axle washers to suit your particular wheels. Do not put on the wheels until later.

The body should be constructed next. There are two sides, a top, a front and a back. Inside, to give it strength, are two body formers.

The formers can be made of ¹⁄₁₆″ wood instead of cardboard, if you choose. The body sides, back and top, may also be built of ¹⁄₁₆″ wood instead of cardboard. Since the front is curved, it should be made only of cardboard. Remember to keep the grain of the cardboard running crosswise, as shown on the plan drawing.

Lay out all the parts of the body full size on your chosen material. Cut out the body formers A and B first. Cut out the windows before you cut the outsides. This will help to keep the wood from splitting and, if you use cardboard, will make the job much easier.

Make certain that the measurements of parts are the same as those given on the plans, especially after you have cut out the pieces. Many times a model maker thinks that it is only necessary to draw the parts correctly on the building material, and that things, naturally, will come out all right. This is not always so. A cut of ¹⁄₃₂″ on either side of the line all around, for instance, will add up to a part actually too small to fit properly. So watch what you do, especially on parts that fit inside something. You will have a hard time making them bigger in order to make them fit!

78

After the two body formers are cut out, check for size and squareness. Next make the rear of the body. This part has two small windows in it. Cut these out very carefully and be certain that they are both the same size as well as square, and the same distance from the top and sides. Then cut the outsides and, if wooden, carefully sandpaper it all.

The two body sides must be exactly alike. You will have to make sure of this or the entire body will come out like a lopsided box that will not fit on the chassis platform. Also check the wheel openings. They must "sit" just outside of the wheel wells.

Cut out the cab window in each body side first. Then do the wheel openings, which are perfectly round.

See that the slope at the body front has the same sloping line as that of the front of the cab windows. Check over everything. Match up the two sides by placing one over the other. If they are not exactly the same trim off where necessary. Keep in mind that the back of the body slopes inward from the belt line to its top.

If your wheel openings are not exactly round, you can fix that now by going around the circular openings with fine sandpaper in your curved X-acto holder to remove any wavy edges. Fine sandpaper, remember, can be used on either wood or cardboard. If you have used cardboard for the body parts, you will have to rub some glue into the cardboard wherever you sandpapered.

When you have finished the two body sides, make the body front. Like the others, the inner windshield section should be the first to be cut out. Do it very carefully. You don't want it to show any unevenness. Next cut the outsides. Now mark out where the lights and the radiator grill go. Curve the front section backward until it matches the slope of the front of the body. Lay it aside.

The next piece to cut out is the top. If possible, make it of wood ¼₆″ thick to give the body added strength. The top is 7″ long and 3⅝″ wide. Bevel the front to match the slope of the windshield and bevel the back slightly to follow the rear body line. Sandpaper it with fine paper placed over your flat X-acto sanding block.

Before you assemble the body permanently, it is a good idea to lay the body together in order to make sure that all the units fit properly. To do this you can use small pins pushed into the parts if they are cardboard, and cellophane tape if wood.

Set your two inside formers A and B in place on the chassis platform. Then fit the two sides. See that they lie against the formers evenly and against the outside of the chassis. Check the position of the wheel openings to see that they are placed correctly and line up with the wheel wells. The front and the rear of the body sides must also match the front and the rear of the chassis.

79

Put the rear of the body in position, then the front. Then lay the roof on. After carefully giving the body a final check to see that it fits accurately, glue the body parts together permanently. Remember that the roof goes on last.

If you decide to put a seat and a steering wheel into the front cab section of the body, do it before placing the roof on. Now is the time also to put in your transparent window material in back of the windshield as well as at the windows.

The steering wheel can be made of $\frac{1}{32}''$-diameter wire bent into a $\frac{3}{4}''$ circle with four cardboard spokes about $\frac{1}{16}''$ wide placed and glued inside it. The steering post is made of dowel $\frac{1}{8}''$ in diameter and about 2'' long.

The steering wheel is glued to one end of the steering post. When they have dried together—and make certain that the steering wheel sits squarely on the post—glue the other end of the steering post to the floor. Place it 1'' in from the left front side, as shown on the plans.

If you make a seat, it is best to carve it out of a block of balsa wood measuring 2'' by 1'' by $1\frac{1}{2}''$. Simply round the front edge of the $1\frac{1}{2}''$ side and slope it gently backward. Sandpaper it smooth and glue it to the floor and to the body form A. Remember that it stands with the rounded $1\frac{1}{2}''$ side upright. See that it clears the wheel wells.

Next you can put the transparent plastic in the windows. You can use any transparent plastic material you wish, but the clear kitchen wrap is probably the easiest to get. Just make sure when you cut out the piece to be glued in back of the window opening that it is $\frac{1}{16}''$ wider than the window itself. This extra width is where you put your glue.

The best way to glue the transparent material to windows and windshield is to first put the glue on one of the edges. Then put the transparency in position. Allow the glue to dry. Then add more glue around the outside and very carefully stretch the clear plastic across the windows and windshield cut-out openings. If you get glue on the clear material, you will have to do the work all over again. Watch how you do the job. Make sure that the material is stretched tightly without creases or wrinkles.

If you want to, you can paint the inside of the cab. This should be done to suit your own taste. A suggested color scheme is all brown with a silver steering post and wheel spokes. The steering wheel rim should be black. Allow all the paint to dry thoroughly. Try not to get paint on either windshield or windows.

Now you can put on the top. It is glued to the top sides, the back and the front of the body. Use enough glue to make certain that it will hold in place securely. Do not allow it to slop over either in the cab or on the outside of the body. Be careful of glue and finger marks. See that the top matches all the body top edges.

Look at the plans to see where the side and back door hinges go. These and the rear center door strip can be made of cardboard $\frac{3}{32}$" wide. Measurements for their lengths are given on the plans. Cut off four for the rear doors and four for each side of the side body doors. Paint them silver along with the rear door center strip, which is shown on the rear view.

The cab door hinges are a bit larger than the others. They are $\frac{3}{16}$" wide and about $\frac{1}{4}$" long. The side view will show you where they go. They are placed at the same spot on both sides of the cab, left and right. These, too, are silver in color. Do not glue the hinges to the body until it is completely painted.

The choice of colors for the exterior, like that of the cab interior, is up to the builder. However, here are a few colors you can use: a bright fire-engine red, light green, bright blue, or medium gray.

After you have removed any pins or cellophane tape that you used to hold the body together while the glue was drying, you should examine the body for pin holes or edges that do not fit together properly. These or any other unwanted openings can be fixed by filling in with model car putty. Use as little as possible and apply it very carefully, never putting any where it does not belong. Allow the putty to dry thoroughly and then add more if necessary, once again allowing it to dry. Then sandpaper it smooth to match the rest of the body. If you rough up any cardboard in the process, you will have to rub glue over those places to even them out and to present a smooth surface for the paint.

By now you know what color you want. Spray enamel is the best to use, but you can also do a good brush job using a soft brush about $1\frac{1}{2}$" wide. Apply the paint a little at a time, on one surface only. Allow the painted surface to lie flat while drying and cover the model with a box to keep dirt away. Repeat the process on all sides. Give it as many coats as necessary in order to obtain a good-looking finish. Indeed, you may even sand down each coat of paint with very fine sandpaper before you put on the next coat. If you choose to do this, try not to go too deeply or you will go into the wood and cardboard. Rubbing each coat will help you get a beautiful finish, but the job will take patience as well as time. In any case, you can put on from two to four coats of paint.

Remember also to be very careful when painting around the windows. If you spray on the paint, you will have to mask them (cover them up) with something—masking tape, for instance—so that the spray does not touch them.

While waiting for the paint to dry, you should make the front and rear bumpers. These are made of cardboard $\frac{7}{16}$" wide and $3\frac{3}{4}$" long. Each end is folded back exactly $\frac{3}{16}$". Note that the cardboard's grain runs from top to bottom. Cut them out carefully and fold the ends back. Then paint them chrome or cover them with kitchen aluminum foil, the kind that comes on a roll. Use Elmer's glue thinned out with a little water to make the foil stick. See that the foil covering is free from wrinkles and creases both before and after it is glued onto the bumpers.

The bumpers go in place at the front and rear of the body, as shown on the plans. Do not put them on until all of the paint and lettering and other decorations have been completed.

When you have the body completely painted, you have to mark out the openings of the cab, side and rear doors. This should be done using a steel straightedge with a semi-soft pencil. Great care must be taken that the lines are drawn on the body accurately. It is best to make some sort of pattern first. Then lightly trace around this pattern and finally mark the door outlines. The more experienced model maker and one who has a very steady hand may do the door outlines with black paint and a very fine brush. Do not try to use inks, for they will run all over the enamel finish.

Most panel trucks that you see on the road have some sort of lettering on the sides. The name of the owner or the company is usually there along with the kind of business engaged in. This kind of truck is used by bakers, plumbers and others, and also by the telephone company as well as fuel oil suppliers for trouble repair units.

You can use your own name on the sides and make up your own company. Letters can be cut out of magazines and glued on with thinned-down Elmer's glue or they can be decals purchased at your model shop. Decals are also sold in various scrolls and decorations, used on many model hot rods. These are excellent for decorations around the lettering. See that anything you put on the body sides is evenly spaced and symmetrical. Both sides should be done in the same manner.

After the lettering is completed, the hinges are put on. Use straight Elmer's glue for this work. It does not mar the finish. Do not use your construction quick-drying glue on anything that is glued to the paint work. Quick-drying glue ruins paint.

You will notice when you look at the plans that there are two rearview mirrors mounted to the sides of the cab. These are made of a disk of aluminum ¼" in diameter. They can be punched out with a ¼"-diameter paper hole punch. Glue them to a pin cut off about ⅝" long. Bend the pin slightly to a curve as shown on the front view. Glue the pin end to the back of the disk. Remember to let the pointed end be free. When the glue has dried, simply insert the pointed end of the pin into the cab, in the position shown on the drawings.

Door handles are simply small pins with the head cut off and with the pointed end bent down about ⅛". These are inserted into the body

82

as the plan illustrates. A $\frac{1}{16}$"-wide strip of cardboard cut to length can be glued with Elmer's glue to the pins, in order to give the door handles more thickness and make them show up better. They are chrome in color.

The windshield wipers are simply two $1\frac{1}{2}$" lengths of wire held in a flat position against the windshield and body with Elmer's glue. Use the glue on the part of the wire that touches the body. Do not get glue on the windshield.

The front grill can be made of strips of aluminum $\frac{1}{16}$" wide for the horizontal bars with several $\frac{1}{4}$" widths placed upright between them. Fit the pieces so they go on the front, as shown. Glue them together, and while they are drying, paint the grill opening flat black. Then, when dry, you can add the completed aluminum grill to the front of the truck. Use Elmer's glue for this.

The two parking lights that go on either side of the grill are made of punched-out $\frac{1}{8}$" aluminum disks, or cardboard disks of the same diameter painted gloss white. The rear stop lights are also $\frac{1}{8}$" disks. These are painted gloss red. Glue them in the positions shown on the front and rear views with a drop of Elmer's glue.

The GMC letters can be cut from some truck ad, or decals can be used. If you are good enough, you can paint on the letters in silver. The gas cap on the driver's side (left) can also be painted on in silver; or you can make a $\frac{1}{4}$" disk and glue it in position.

Other details that you may want to add and that you have noticed on real trucks or in magazine advertisements should be added now.

Next you can put the wheels on. They are slipped over the axles so that they touch the washers. A hub cap can be made from a piece of wood drilled out in the center to match the diameter of the axles. Then the outside of the wood is rounded, sandpapered, painted chrome, and glued in place.

Another method used to hold the wheels on is to wind thread or fine wire around the axles and glue it so that it holds in position. When the glue has dried, chrome paint goes on. The simplest method is the use of glue in a rather large drop on the axle end. When dry, this drop of glue is also painted chrome.

In any case, you must be very careful that you do not allow any glue to touch the wheels, for this will prevent them from turning around. And you must see that the wheels are fixed tightly enough against the washers so that they revolve without wiggling in and out.

Lastly, put the bumpers in place, using Elmer's glue. See that they are fastened tightly and are square to the body as well as in the same horizontal line. The plans will show you exactly how they are placed. This finishes your panel delivery truck model.

Chapter 9

The 1910 Bucket Seat Racing Car

By now you have had enough experience constructing models to build something more detailed. We have chosen this 1910 racing car for our next effort because it embodies a good amount of detail and because, being an early automobile, it has no compounded curves to be made. Nor are there vast expanses of sheet metal to try to duplicate and keep free from waves and hollow spots.

You can still have an excellent model of this car without including all details. Such things, for instance, as separate steering knuckles can be "faked" in one piece with the axle; and the radius rods for the rear axles can be omitted, as well as the underpan. The hood strap can be left off, and you don't have to put louvers on the hood sides.

On the other hand, it must be remembered that a good model maker always tries to put as many of the original details into his work as he can, and to make his model as authentic as possible. Often the reason for simplifying is lack of materials or time.

Racing cars, like this 1910 automobile, were very expensive. These cars were sometimes fitted out for road work, and were used by some owners as their regular everyday cars. Then they were called sports cars instead of racing machines. They had added equipment such as fenders and running boards, headlights, tail-lights and sometimes small cowl lights. On one or both running boards, tool boxes

- DETAILS -

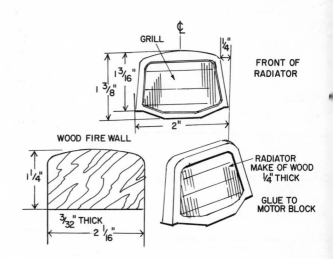

GRILL

FRONT OF
RADIATOR

1 $\frac{3}{16}$ "

1 $\frac{3}{8}$ "

$\frac{1}{4}$ "

2 "

WOOD FIRE WALL

RADIATOR
MAKE OF WOOD
$\frac{1}{4}$ " THICK

GLUE TO
MOTOR BLOCK

1 $\frac{1}{4}$ "

$\frac{3}{32}$ " THICK

2 $\frac{1}{16}$ "

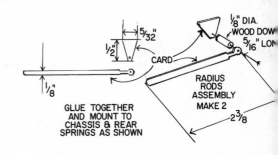

$\frac{5}{32}$ "

$\frac{1}{2}$ "

$\frac{1}{8}$ " DIA.
WOOD DOW

$\frac{5}{16}$ " LON

CARD

RADIUS
RODS
ASSEMBLY
MAKE 2

$\frac{1}{8}$ "

2 $\frac{3}{8}$

GLUE TOGETHER
AND MOUNT TO
CHASSIS & REAR
SPRINGS AS SHOWN

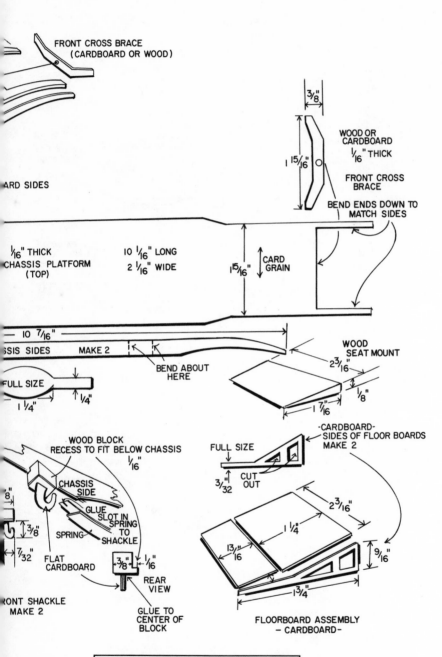

FRONT CROSS BRACE
(CARDBOARD OR WOOD)

$\frac{3}{8}$"

WOOD OR
CARDBOARD
$\frac{1}{16}$" THICK

$1\frac{15}{16}$"

FRONT CROSS
BRACE

BEND ENDS DOWN TO
MATCH SIDES

ARD SIDES

$\frac{1}{16}$" THICK   10 $\frac{1}{16}$" LONG
CHASSIS PLATFORM   2 $\frac{1}{16}$" WIDE
(TOP)

$1\frac{15}{16}$"   CARD
GRAIN

10 $\frac{7}{16}$"

SSIS SIDES   MAKE 2

BEND ABOUT
HERE

WOOD
SEAT MOUNT

2$\frac{3}{16}$"

$\frac{1}{8}$"

FULL SIZE

$\frac{1}{4}$"

1 $\frac{1}{4}$"

1 $\frac{7}{16}$"

WOOD BLOCK
RECESS TO FIT BELOW CHASSIS

$\frac{1}{16}$"

FULL SIZE

CARDBOARD-
SIDES OF FLOOR BOARDS
MAKE 2

CHASSIS
SIDE

GLUE
SLOT IN
SPRING
TO
SHACKLE

$\frac{3}{32}$"   CUT
OUT

2$\frac{3}{16}$"

SPRING

8"

$\frac{3}{8}$"

FLAT
CARDBOARD

$\frac{7}{32}$"

$\frac{3}{8}$" $\frac{1}{16}$"

REAR
VIEW

1 $\frac{1}{4}$"

$\frac{13}{16}$"

$\frac{9}{16}$"

RONT SHACKLE
MAKE 2

GLUE TO
CENTER OF
BLOCK

1 $\frac{3}{4}$"

FLOORBOARD ASSEMBLY
– CARDBOARD –

1910 RACING CAR

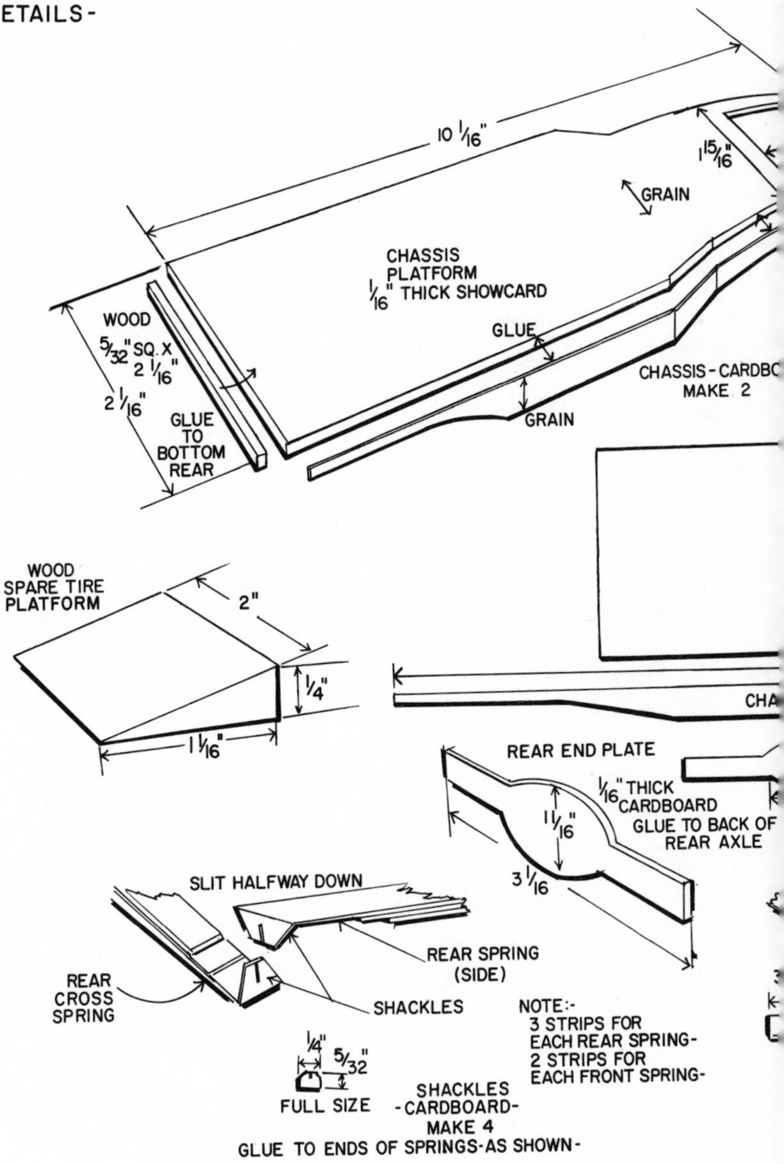

10 $\frac{1}{16}$"

1 $\frac{15}{16}$"

GRAIN

CHASSIS
PLATFORM
$\frac{1}{16}$" THICK SHOWCARD

GLUE

WOOD
$\frac{5}{32}$" SQ. X
2 $\frac{1}{16}$"

2 $\frac{1}{16}$"

GLUE
TO
BOTTOM
REAR

GRAIN

CHASSIS-CARDBO
MAKE 2

WOOD
SPARE TIRE
PLATFORM

2"

$\frac{1}{4}$"

1 $\frac{1}{16}$"

CHA

REAR END PLATE

$\frac{1}{16}$" THICK
CARDBOARD
GLUE TO BACK OF
REAR AXLE

1 $\frac{1}{16}$"

3 $\frac{1}{16}$"

SLIT HALFWAY DOWN

REAR SPRING
(SIDE)

REAR
CROSS
SPRING

SHACKLES

NOTE:-
3 STRIPS FOR
EACH REAR SPRING-
2 STRIPS FOR
EACH FRONT SPRING-

$\frac{1}{4}$" $\frac{5}{32}$"

FULL SIZE

SHACKLES
-CARDBOARD-
MAKE 4
GLUE TO ENDS OF SPRINGS·AS SHOWN-

F

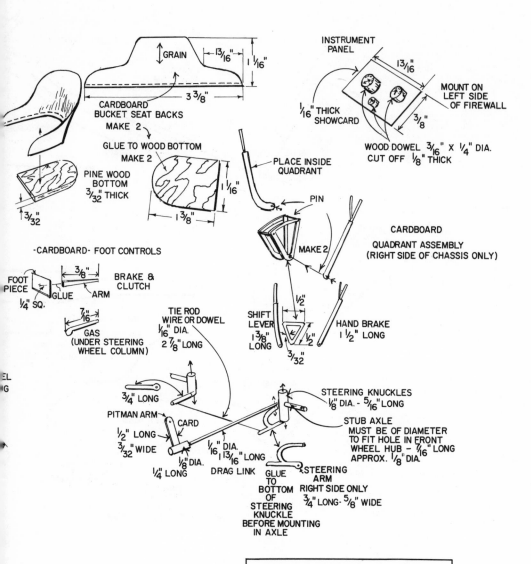

GRAIN
13/16"
1 1/16"
3 3/8"
CARDBOARD
BUCKET SEAT BACKS
MAKE 2

INSTRUMENT PANEL
13/16"
MOUNT ON LEFT SIDE OF FIREWALL
1/16" THICK SHOWCARD
3/8"

GLUE TO WOOD BOTTOM
MAKE 2

PLACE INSIDE QUADRANT

WOOD DOWEL 3/16" X 1/4" DIA. CUT OFF 1/8" THICK

PINE WOOD BOTTOM 3/32" THICK
1 1/16"
3/32"
1 3/8"

PIN

CARDBOARD
QUADRANT ASSEMBLY
(RIGHT SIDE OF CHASSIS ONLY)

-CARDBOARD- FOOT CONTROLS

MAKE 2

FOOT PIECE
1/4" SQ.
3/8"
GLUE
ARM
BRAKE & CLUTCH

SHIFT LEVER 1 3/8" LONG
1/2"
1/2"
3/32"

HAND BRAKE 1 1/2" LONG

7/16"
GAS
(UNDER STEERING WHEEL COLUMN)

TIE ROD WIRE OR DOWEL 1/16" DIA. 2 7/8" LONG

EL NG

3/4" LONG

STEERING KNUCKLES 1/8" DIA. - 5/16" LONG

PITMAN ARM
CARD
1/2" LONG
3/32" WIDE
1/8" DIA.
1/4" LONG

1/16" DIA. 1 13/16" LONG

STUB AXLE
MUST BE OF DIAMETER TO FIT HOLE IN FRONT WHEEL HUB – 7/16" LONG APPROX. 1/8" DIA.

DRAG LINK

GLUE TO BOTTOM OF STEERING KNUCKLE BEFORE MOUNTING IN AXLE

STEERING ARM
RIGHT SIDE ONLY
3/4" LONG - 5/8" WIDE

1910 RACING CAR

Note the details possible to include in this model of a cardboard and plastic racing car. (*Kirt Miska*)

were found which in those days carried all the different sizes of wrenches, screwdrivers, tire irons, tire patches, tire valves, tape, extra wire, and fuses that the box could hold; and of course, a hand tire pump!

Also to be found on the running board or just below it, fastened to the side of the chassis, was a small capsule-shaped brass oil tank. Coming out from the back, just below the rear axle, was usually a very large exhaust stack. A muffler cut-out helped to make the car go faster and rattled houses with its loud noise as the car roared past. The cut-out simply cut out the effect of the muffler which was placed on the car to silence the exhaust of the engine. For simplicity's sake neither the cut-out nor the exhaust pipe is shown on the plans. You can add the exhaust pipe if you wish after the underpan has been put in place. It is a simple piece of wood dowel ¼″ in diameter and is glued below the rear axle and to the inside of the underpan.

When you look at the plan, and look at all details before you start, you will notice that the car is constructed on a platform-type chassis. This kind of model chassis makes it unnecessary to use any cross-members and does not require flooring. It is also easy, with this type chassis, to mark off the position of the various parts to be placed on it.

Probably the things that you will find hardest to make are the spring shackles for the back of the front springs and for the front of the rear springs, the front axle assembly, and perhaps the radiator. A close study of the plans and the instructions will see you through this, helped by your own determination to make a good model that you know will turn out to be a prize.

Only the top view, side view, front view and rear view of this car are to scale (¾ inch to 1 foot). Detail sketches are not drawn to scale and are shown only to assist the builder in seeing shapes and methods of construction. This is true not only for this racing car model but also for most scale models.

The chassis is the first unit to be built. It consists of the platform or top and two sides. The two sides are exactly the same. Trace out the side members of the chassis, one for the right side and one for the left side. Then cut out the top of the chassis. Be sure that all lines are even and square to each other and that if a center line were drawn through the top both sides would be exactly the same if the top were folded along this center line.

Either wood or cardboard may be used for the chassis. You may use a combination of both—wood for the top and cardboard for the side members, or the other way around. Wood should be about $\frac{1}{16}''$ thick and can be balsa, pine or bass wood.

No list of materials is given for this model. The builder by now should be able to judge what he needs either before he starts or certainly as he goes along.

When the chassis parts have been cut out, they should be carefully sandpapered. Keep the curved under-section of the front and rear of the side members to an even flowing arch, free of nicks or waves.

The rivets that are shown on the chassis side members may be simulated by inserting very small pinheads at the places shown. A spot of glue will hold them. It is best to use the quick-drying glue.

In order to support the wheels and axles, the chassis has springs. However, instead of just four springs, as is normal, this 1910 car has five. Three springs are at the rear and two are at the front. Note where they are placed by taking a careful look at the drawings.

At the front end of the chassis, two normal half-elliptic type springs are used. The model springs are made up of shirt cardboard cut in strips for the leaves. The front strips are $\frac{1}{8}''$ wide and the rear strips are $\frac{5}{32}''$ wide. Build up each spring by gluing several leaves (strips) of cardboard on top of each other until a thickness of about $\frac{1}{8}''$ is reached. This $\frac{1}{8}''$ thickness may have to be arrived at by gluing two, three or more leaves (strips) together, depending on the kind of cardboard you use. Remember to make each strip, or leaf, at least $\frac{1}{4}''$ shorter at each end than the one above it. Keep in mind that the measurements given for the spring lengths are for the longest leaf only.

Glue the spring leaves together—five in all. They should have a slight bow to them, as shown on the side view of the chassis. This shape is put in before and after you glue the spring leaves together, and it must be done before the springs are mounted to the chassis. Simply bow each leaf before assembly and then again after they are glued together.

Each spring is fastened to the chassis by shackles. The front springs are glued at their front ends to the front arch of the chassis side members as shown on the three-view plan. The front springs' rear ends are glued to C-shaped shackles. These shackles are made of small pieces of cardboard or aluminum. The plan details will show you their construction. Make two—one for each side. Glue these shackles to the rear of the longest leaf of each front spring (the top one) and also to the bottom of each side member of the chassis. Behind the side member, glue a block of wood as described in the detail sketches to help hold the shackles in place. Allow the assembly to dry thoroughly. Make certain that both springs are an equal distance away from the chassis.

The rear spring assembly is made of two side springs and the rear cross-spring. Make certain that you use the two $3\frac{1}{8}''$-long springs for the sides and the shorter, $2\frac{11}{16}''$ spring, for the rear. The shackles are rather simple, being four small bits of cardboard or aluminum cut to the shape shown on the plans. The detail drawing explains how they go together. Carefully slip each shackle into its matching piece and glue together. When the glue has dried, glue them once again to the ends of the three springs. Remember that the cross-spring goes upside down, with the longest spring leaf at the bottom. The side springs have the longest leaf at the top.

The rear spring is glued to a piece of $\frac{5}{32}''$-square wood which in turn is glued to the rear underside of the chassis platform. The fronts of the rear side springs are attached to shackles built of dowel $\frac{1}{8}''$ in diameter, $\frac{1}{4}''$ long. Simply glue the dowel very securely to the chassis side in the position shown. Make certain that the spring end will touch it when the spring assembly is in place. Or, you can put a hole in the chassis side frame on each side and run a single length of $\frac{1}{8}''$ dowel through so that the dowel sticks out $\frac{1}{4}''$ on both sides. Glue in position.

As one unit, glue the three rear springs to the two side shackles ($\frac{1}{8}''$-diameter dowels) and to the center of the $\frac{5}{32}''$-square cross-piece at the rear of the chassis. Set the chassis down on your flat working surface and check it to make certain that all springs touch the board and that the chassis is level at all angles. If not, adjust by flattening or putting more bow in the springs. Be careful that you do not snap anything off.

The radius rods on either side of the rear of the chassis are constructed now. They are built of cardboard and a short length of $\frac{1}{8}$"-diameter dowel cut to a length of $\frac{5}{16}$". When you have cut the dowels, cut out two triangular pieces and two rods as shown on the detail sketches of the plans.

First, glue the dowels to the lower part of the triangular piece, one unit for each side. Allow the glue to dry and then add the rods to the dowel. Use enough glue to make certain that the finished units are held together well. Allow them to dry thoroughly.

While the radius rods are drying, make the rear axle. It is a simple affair, consisting of a $\frac{3}{16}$"-diameter dowel, about 4" long. To the back of this dowel, a cardboard dummy rear end housing is glued. This can be seen on the rear view of the car. It should be cut out after tracing it onto a smooth cardboard piece. However, you must remember that its ends will fit between the inside of the rear wheels allowing $\frac{1}{64}$" clearance so that it does not actually touch either of the wheels. Make it so that each end is at least $1\frac{3}{4}$" from the center, and trim the ends off later on.

The wheels that go on the axles should be purchased. Or perhaps you may have a set left over from a $\frac{3}{4}$" scale plastic kit. The four wheels should be 2" in diameter. The wheels must have 12 spokes to be authentic. The front spokes are thinner than the rear, and the rear wheels should have the brake drums fixed to them as part of the wheel itself. The Old-Timer Aurora kits have perfect wheels to fit this model.

If by some chance you cannot purchase the wheels, you can make them of several 2"-diameter disks glued together until they acquire a thickness of $\frac{1}{4}$". Make four and round the edges so as to give a "tire" shape, as shown on the front and rear views. Paint on your tire with flat black paint. It should be $\frac{5}{16}$" wide all around. Inside this you can draw 12 spokes on each side of the wheel and paint them in any color you wish. Remember to make a black disk in the center of the rear wheels, $\frac{7}{8}$" in diameter, to represent the rear brake drums.

Make the center, or hub, of the wheel $\frac{3}{8}$" in diameter and drill a $\frac{1}{8}$"-diameter hole through it at the wheel's center.

The plastic wheels also have these approximate measurements. You will have to cut down the ends of the back axle so that it will have the same diameter as the hole drilled in your home-made wheel hub or the one in any purchased wheel set.

After the rear axle (dowel) has had its ends trimmed to fit the wheel hubs, just as shown on the top view, you can slip the rear wheels on and see if all is proper. The wheels should turn freely, but not wobble.

Place the dummy rear end housing against the axle and see how much you have to trim off in order to get it to fit between the wheels, as described in the preceding paragraphs. Glue it to the rear axle, as shown on the rear view of the plans.

If you look at the side view, you can see how the rear axle goes and the position of the dummy rear axle housing. Now glue the rear axle to the bottom center of the rear springs. You may hold it in place by wrapping some sewing thread around axle and spring. Use enough to hold it securely in position. Make certain that the axle extends the same distance from each side of the chassis and that it is in the same line across as the chassis when viewed from the rear.

Now take your radius rods and glue them in place, one on each side. The triangular piece goes on the chassis side and the end of the rod against the front of the rear axle. The top and side views will show you its position. Looking at it from the side, it should be perfectly horizontal with the chassis. Wait until the front axle is in place before putting the rear wheel on.

You can either make the front axle in one piece or build it up of separate pieces. The latter is the more accurate, though it may be somewhat harder. If it is to be one piece, you need only cut it out of ¼″-thick and ¾″-wide pine or bass wood, without making the cutout for the steering knuckles, as shown on the front view. This way, only the stub axles need be made separately. These stub axles should be dowel of the correct diameter to fit your front wheels, if purchased (usually ⅛″ in diameter). The two stub axles are about ⁷⁄₁₆″ long. If you have made your own wheels, simply drill a ⅛″ hole in the hub to take the stub axle.

If you intend to build the axles of separate pieces, then cut out the front axle from the same size pine or bass wood piece ¼″ thick by ¾″ wide. After you have it shaped and sandpapered, and have made certain that each side is exactly the same as the other, very carefully cut out the section at each end where the steering knuckles will go. Sandpaper the entire axle smooth and see that both ends are alike.

It is useful to make an aluminum template finished to the size and shape of the axle as seen on the front view to use as a guide in cutting out the axle. If you do this, it is suggested that you use a fine jeweler's blade in your jig saw. Allow about ¹⁄₆₄″ between the cut and the exact outline. Finish it with sandpaper, or a fine pattern file.

Each of the steering knuckles is made of two small dowels. The dowel that represents the knuckle itself is the upright one, while the other, horizontal, is the stub axle.

The length for the steering knuckle (dowel) is ⁵⁄₁₆″. It is ⅛″ in diameter. The length of the stub axle, as mentioned before, is ⁷⁄₁₆″.

Before you put the steering knuckles in position, glue the stub axle to them at their exact center. It will form a T stood on end. Use plenty of glue to ensure a very strong bond, but make certain that you don't get any more than ¹⁄₁₆″ down the axle or it will interfere with the placement of the front wheels.

Allow the axle-steering knuckle assembly to dry thoroughly. When the glue has dried, add the steering arms, which take the tie rod, to the bottom of each knuckle. The right-hand one has a U shape and takes the long drag link as well as the tie rod, but the left steering arm is plain.

Trace each one onto a piece of cardboard or thin aluminum and carefully cut it out. Glue them to the bottom of the steering knuckles, as shown on the plans. Make certain that they are so placed that when the stub axles face outward, right and left, the steering arms face the back. Allow everything to dry before going farther.

Now place each steering knuckle inside one of the hollows at the ends of the front axle. Do not force them in. If you have made the hollow too small, either take off a bit of the knuckle at the top or trim off some of the inside of the hollow. Work carefully until a snug fit is obtained. Make certain that, when the knuckles are in position, the stub axles line up when you look at them from the front. If they do not, one wheel will be lower than the other and the car will not stand on its wheels properly.

The tie rod goes on the front axle assembly next. This is a piece of wire, or dowel, $\frac{1}{16}''$ in diameter and $2\frac{7}{8}''$ long. Simply cut it to length and glue it to the top of the steering arms, as shown in the detail drawing. Glue the axle to the bottom of the front springs in the same way as you fastened the rear axle to the rear springs.

Joining the U-shaped steering arm to the side of the chassis is the drag rod or drag link. Make it of two sizes of dowel and a piece of cardboard or aluminum. A dowel $1\frac{13}{16}''$ long and $\frac{1}{16}''$ in diameter is used for the front of the arm and a piece of $\frac{1}{8}''$-diameter dowel $\frac{1}{4}''$ long is used for the rear. Glue them together. When dry, add the Pitman or steering arm, as shown. It is $\frac{1}{2}''$ long and $\frac{3}{32}''$ wide. Round the top and taper the sides a little before gluing in place.

When the Pitman arm is dry, put it in position and see that it touches the U-shaped steering arm and the side of the chassis, as shown on the top and side views in the detail drawing. If correct, glue it in place. Place all four wheels on the axles. Set the chassis on a flat surface. All wheels must touch the ground and the chassis must line up evenly on both sides and at the front and rear. The wheels may be a bit sloppy now in their fit, but later on, when you put the hub caps in place, they will hold properly. Corrections to the chassis, in order to make it stand properly, should be made now. Either adjust the springs or insert bits of cardboard between the axle and the bottom of the springs. You will have to cut the glue away to do this.

When the chassis sits the way it should, you are ready to put on the underpan. This is a simple job. Cut two pieces of cardboard, one for the front of the underpan which ends just below the fire wall, and one for the rear which ends about $\frac{1}{2}''$ in front of the rear axle.

The two sections of the underpan snap in between the side chassis members and touch the bottom of the chassis floor. The underpan is not indicated on either front or rear view drawings, in order to keep these views as simple as possible.

Measure out a piece of cardboard 2¾″ long, 3″ wide at one end and 2½″ wide at the other end—a sort of shallow triangle. Cut it out and snap it between the side members. It should slant slightly downward toward the rear. Trim the edges until it shows ⅜″ below the bottom of the chassis sides. Also trim the front and rear ends so that they appear straight up and down. Note that on the side view drawing the front of the under pan just touches the front chassis cross-brace. This cross-brace is located below the radiator.

Cut another piece of cardboard out for the rear section of the under pan. It is 3″ wide and about 4¾″ long. Snap it in place so that the front end fits against the rear of the front section. Trim it to fit so that ⅜″ shows below the bottom of the chassis side members. Trim the front to fit closely against the rear of the front section. Cut the rear so that it appears to slant upward toward the rear, as the side view shows. When the two sections are correctly fitted, glue them in place.

Trace out the front cross-brace. For a look at its shape, see the front view. This piece may be made of either hard wood 1⁄16″ thick or cardboard or aluminum. Cut it to shape. Make it so that the ends are a bit longer than is shown on the front-view drawing—about 2⅛″ long. Trim off the ends a little at a time until it fits snugly between the insides of the chassis side members.

When you get it to fit properly, glue it in position, almost exactly below the front of the radiator. You can see where it goes by looking at the side-view plan. After this cross-brace has dried in place, you are ready to cut out the radiator and proceed with the rest of the units that go on the top of the chassis.

All measurements for the radiator as well as its shape will be found in the drawings. Make it from a piece of hard balsa or pine wood. Cut out a template of aluminum and use this as your guide so that you will obtain the same shape on both sides.

Cut out the radiator with either a jeweler's blade fitted in your jig saw or by making straight saw cuts about its edges 1⁄16″ from the final outline with your X-acto razor-back saw. After you have roughed it out, sandpaper the edges very carefully, still using the template as a guide, until the exact outline has been obtained. Use the drawings and reverse the template against the radiator as your check for accuracy.

Now that you have the outline cut to size, mark off the inside in pencil for the radiator grill outline. Then fill in the outline with flat black paint or black cardboard. Leave the rest plain until later. If you wish, however, and can be very careful during assembly, you can now paint the rest of the radiator brass. Glue the radiator to the chassis in the position shown on the plans. Make certain that it is upright as well as square to the chassis. Make the radiator cap of $\frac{3}{16}$"-diameter cardboard disks glued to a $\frac{1}{8}$" length of $\frac{3}{16}$"-diameter wood dowel. Glue it to the top center of the radiator. It is brass-colored.

The firewall is made next from a piece of pine wood $\frac{3}{32}$" thick, $2\frac{1}{16}$" wide, and $1\frac{1}{4}$" high. While the bottom and the edges are straight, the top is arched gently. It is a good idea also to make a template for this firewall and cut out around it. Make sure that the arch is accurate and that both sides of its curve are the same. The arch, in this case, can be sandpapered to shape without the need of sawing.

Mount the firewall to the chassis so that it is $2\frac{3}{8}$" behind the radiator, measuring from the front of the radiator. Like the radiator, it must stand exactly upright and square across the chassis. Glue it in place securely.

Between the radiator and the firewall is the hood that covers the engine. Since this model car does not have an engine, one possible way to make the hood is with a solid block of balsa wood. If you wish to do this, fit a block $1\frac{3}{16}$" high between the firewall and the rear of the radiator. Trace the outline of the radiator on one end. Turn the block around and trace the radiator outline on the other end. Then, using your X-acto knife, shave the block down until the top arch shape is almost to the traced line, and the sides, which slope away, are almost finished. Then complete the job with sandpaper.

You can draw 16 louvers on each side of the hood or leave it plain, as you wish. Put a piece of $\frac{1}{16}$"-thick wood alongside the hood block in the width and shape of the chassis top, as shown on the plans. Glue this $\frac{1}{16}$"-thick wood to the chassis between the firewall and the back of the radiator. Make certain that the hood block lines up with the rear of the radiator. Allow it to dry in place and then draw a center line down the top to represent the hinge.

Another way to make the hood is to cut a piece of cardboard about $2\frac{1}{8}$" wide and about 4" long. With the grain of the cardboard running in the direction of the width, carefully bend the cardboard until the shape follows the contour (or outline) of the radiator. Trim it to fit and add a piece of cardboard or $\frac{1}{16}$"-thick wood, shaped like the radiator, above the chassis top line and inside both ends of the cardboard hood. These two radiator-shaped pieces hold the hood to shape and add strength. You can draw 16 louvers on each side and the line that represents the hinge on the top center before you glue the hood in position.

Regardless of which method of hood-making you use, you still must place the $\frac{1}{16}$"-thick wood piece on the chassis top between the radiator and the firewall, as described a few paragraphs before.

One other way to construct the hood also makes use of the card-

A combination of cardboard and plastic parts from a kit makes a realistic racing car that's fun to work on. (*Kirt Miska*)

board method. This time the cardboard is made wider—2⅜″—and incorporates the radiator top and sides as well. It is made as described in the previous paragraph. The difference is that the cardboard bulkhead that is placed at the front is drawn full-length to the exact outline of the whole radiator, while the rear bulkhead radiator outline is cut off at the chassis top.

When the radiator-hood unit is completed, you must draw a line ¼″ in from the front to represent the side width of the radiator and lines for the louvers and top hinge as well. The finished hood is glued in position to the firewall and the 1/16″-thick piece that goes at the bottom of the hood sides.

The floorboard assembly rests against the bottom rear of the firewall on top of the chassis and goes back to the seat wedge. This consists of the floorboards themselves and two supporting side pieces.

To make it, first trace out the side pieces on 1/16″ wood or pieces of cardboard or aluminum. If they are to be made of wood, use your X-acto knife to do the job and a steel straightedge to help you keep clean, straight lines. Use scissors if you make it of cardboard. If you use a fairly heavy aluminum, cut it with a jeweler's blade in your jig saw and file off the roughness until even lines have been achieved.

The first thing to do when constructing the floorboard side pieces is to cut out the two hollow sections indicated on the side view.

93

All cutting of wood or cardboard can be done in the normal way, but if you use aluminum, you will have to drill a hole in the center of the cutout of each side large enough for your jeweler's blade to go through. Pass the blade through the hole, reinsert the blade into its frame, and cut the aluminum away. Then remove the excess with an X-acto flat pattern file until you have clean, straight lines. Next cut the outsides to shape.

The side pieces are glued in position on the chassis with the hollowed-out portions facing forward. They go in place above the chassis side members.

On top of the side pieces is the floorboard. This should be made in two sections, front and rear. Both are the width of the chassis. The front board measures about 1⅛" from the firewall to the bottom and the rear board measures 1³⁄₁₆" from the rear forward.

Make the floorboards of either cardboard or wood. If you make them of wood, do not use material thicker than ¹⁄₁₆". The front floorboard overlaps the rear floorboard where they touch. Drill a ⅛"-diameter hole in the front floorboard for the steering column. Look at the plans, side and top views, to see this. The floorboards are glued in place.

Right behind the floorboards is the wooden seat wedge. On this wedge are mounted the two bucket seats. The wedge can be made of pine, bass or hard balsa wood. It is the full width of the chassis and is 1⁷⁄₁₆" long. The wood you use must have a thickness of ⅛" in order to obtain the correct angle for the wedge.

Simply sand it down so that it is wedge-shaped, one end coming almost to a knife-edge. The other is left ⅛" thick. Check your work and make sure that the seat wedge is level and square. If it is not properly made, the seats will not "sit" correctly. Glue the wedge in place so that the ⅛"-thick end fits against the rear of the floorboards.

In order to construct the two bucket seats, you will have to make a wraparound back and a bottom, which can be of pine wood, ³⁄₃₂" thick. The seat backs can be either cardboard or thin aluminum.

The detail drawings show the seat backs and the bottoms. Full-size parts can be obtained by enlarging the patterns to the measurements given on the drawings. Cut out the seat bottoms first. Make certain that the curved part is accurate, having the same radius at each side. Lay the two seat bottoms on top of each other and check to see that they are both the same. Set them aside after you have sandpapered all around their edges.

Now cut out the backs. Here, too, you must be sure that both sides are exactly alike and that both seat backs match each other perfectly. Make certain that the grain runs up and down if the backs are made of cardboard.

When the backs have been cut out, carefully curve them with

your fingers until they fit around the wooden bottoms. The edges of the sides and bottoms must line up so that the seats will be the same at both sides. Glue the sides to the bottoms. Hold the units together with small pins until the glue is dry.

Before you mount the seats, you may wish to put some sort of upholstery on them. This can be done by gluing some very thin leather to the inside of the backs and folding the leather over the top edges so that it runs about ⅛" wide all around. The side view will give you an idea of how it should look. However, you might not want to cover the edges. Then all you have to do is trim the leather off at the upper edge of the seat backs.

On the seat bottoms, glue a bit of cotton to the inside. Then cut a pattern of leather a bit larger than the bottoms and glue it over the cotton and to the inner edges where the backs and bottoms meet. If you do not upholster, cut a balsa piece ¼" thick to fit over the seat bottoms to represent the seats.

Be very careful with the glue. Do not get any on your fingers or on the top of the leather. It will spoil the seats. Usually, on the real cars, the seats were cherry-red in color, but tan, brown or black can be used. Now glue the completed seats in place over the seat wedge. The front of the seat bottoms should go ⅛" back from the wedge's front. Both seats should touch each other along the chassis center line.

Behind the seats are two tanks. These carried gasoline in the real car. Since our model does not, the tanks do not need to be hollow. The large tank can be made from a length of dowel 1¾₆" in diameter. This one can be made from a piece cut from an old broomstick, if you can find one that has the correct diameter. If not, you can purchase a large-diameter dowel stick at any good hardware store, or, of course, you can carve it out of a block of balsa wood using an X-acto knife and sandpaper. The tank must be perfectly round and have a smooth surface.

The smaller tank, that goes back of the large one, is made of 1¹⁄₁₆"-diameter wood dowel or the nearest to that size that you can buy, or you can make it yourself out of balsa wood. In either case, the length of each tank is the width of the chassis. If you can find cardboard tubes of the correct sizes, they can be used instead of wood dowels, but then you must close up the ends with cardboard disks.

On the top of each tank at its center is a filler cap. These caps are made of cardboard disks. They are built up to a height of ⅛". The large filler cap is ⅜" in diameter and the small one is ¼". Cut out and glue together several disks until the correct height has been reached. Make sure that the disks are round and lie exactly on top of each other. When the disks have dried together, sandpaper the edges if they need it and glue them in place on the tanks.

The tanks are glued to the top of the chassis. The seat backs

This model is similar to the one for which building instructions are given. The scale is ¾ inch to 1 foot. (*Kirt Miska*)

just clear the large front tank by about $\frac{1}{32}$". The small tank fits in behind the larger one. Make certain that they are in line across the chassis and that the filler caps are upright. Each end of the tanks should be even with the chassis side members.

The straps going around the tanks, at their ends, are made of $\frac{1}{8}$"-wide paper strips which can be glued in place so that they appear like the straps indicated on the side view.

Back of the small tank is the spare-wheel platform. This, like the piece below the seats, is a wedge made of wood. It is 1" wide and 2" long. Make it from wood $\frac{1}{4}$" thick, just as you made the seat wedge. It must be square and smooth all along its surface. Hard balsa will do, or pine wood. Cut the blank out and sandpaper to the wedge shape. Smooth off with fine sandpaper and then glue it in position so that the point lines up with the rear of the chassis, as you can see by looking at the top view of the drawings.

Now we are ready for the steering wheel assembly, hand levers, foot pedals and instrument board.

Let's start with the foot pedals. They are made of cardboard, cut out as shown on the detail drawings. The brake and clutch pedals are the same. One goes to the right of the steering column and one to the left. Cut the $\frac{1}{4}$"-square piece for the foot piece and a $\frac{1}{16}$"-wide piece, $\frac{3}{8}''$ long, for the arm. Center the arm back of the foot piece and glue them together. When the glue is dry, mount them in position on the floorboard where you see them located on the top-view drawing.

The gas pedal is simply a piece of cardboard strip about $\frac{3}{32}''$ wide and $\frac{7}{16}''$ long. Cut it out and bend one end so that it is curved downward slightly. Glue the straight end to the floorboard below where the steering column will go—just between the clutch and brake pedals and slightly lower.

It is best to buy the steering wheel. Like the plastic wheels, the steering wheel may be found in a kit, or you may be able to get it at the model shop. A steering wheel that is just about right for our racing car model will be found in some plastic Old-Timer Aurora kits.

If you have to construct a steering wheel, take a piece of heavy brass wire $\frac{3}{32}''$ in diameter and curve it to a $1\frac{1}{16}''$-diameter circle. Next cut out four spokes $\frac{1}{16}''$ wide, of either cardboard or wood, and place them inside the wire circle. See that the ends of the wire circle touch. Glue the four spokes to the inside of the wire circle in the form of a cross. The spokes need not be slanted as they are shown on the side view but can be put in place flat.

It is a good idea to draw out the steering wheel full size on a piece of wood or paper and to build up the wheel right over your drawing. Make certain that the spokes are at right angles to each other and are glued securely to each other and the rim. Have one of the spokes touch the split of the wire rim. This way the glue from the end of the spoke will help hold the rim from parting. Pins can be used, placed around the rim, to assist in keeping everything in place until the glue has dried thoroughly.

The steering column is made from a $2\frac{1}{2}''$-long length of wood dowel, $\frac{1}{8}''$ in diameter. Cut it to length and sandpaper the wood until it is smooth. Now, carefully insert the steering column into the $\frac{1}{8}''$ hole in the front floorboard. The end inserted into the floorboard should be pushed down so that it touches the firewall. The other end should stand about $1\frac{1}{16}''$ above the floorboard. Glue it securely in position. Be careful not to get glue on the floorboard. Place a length of wood beneath the upright end of the steering column to help hold it at the correct angle until the glue has dried.

You can wrap and glue a piece of paper around the steering column where it touches the floorboard to represent the holding bracket, as shown on the side and top views.

Next, assemble the instrument panel. This is made of $\frac{1}{16}''$ wood. It measures $1\frac{3}{16}''$ by $\frac{3}{8}''$. Cut it out and sandpaper it with fine sandpaper. Then cut three $\frac{1}{8}''$ pieces from a $\frac{1}{4}''$-diameter wood dowel stick. Do this with your X-acto razor-back fine-tooth saw. You must have a clean cut without splintered edges. Sandpaper the pieces and glue them to the instrument panel. These are your dials. The faces may be painted white and small hands drawn on them. The detail drawing and the side and top views will give you any further information you need for this assembly. When completed, glue it in position against the right side of the firewall $\frac{1}{16}''$ down from the top and $\frac{1}{4}''$ in from the edge. Place a small bit of wood, $\frac{1}{8}''$ thick, back of it, and glue it to the instrument panel and the firewall. This will give the instrument panel its upward tilt, as you will see when you consult the side-view drawing.

The last detail for the controls is the hand lever assembly. This consists of a quadrant and the shift and brake levers. All can be made of cardboard. First draw the two quadrant pieces on cardboard. (The quadrants are simply triangles with their centers cut out. They measure $1\frac{1}{2}''$ wide at the top and $\frac{1}{2}''$ long at their sides.)

Cut out the centers first with a sharp X-acto knife. Use a steel straightedge as your guide. Allow at least $\frac{3}{32}''$ between the edge of the cut-out centers and the outer edge of the quadrant. When the centers have been cut out, lay your straightedge against the cardboard. Hold the straightedge down securely and trim the outside of each quadrant to shape. Before you join the two quadrant sides together, make the hand levers. The shift lever is $1\frac{1}{4}''$ long and about $\frac{3}{32}''$ wide. The brake lever is $\frac{1}{16}''$ wide and $1\frac{1}{2}''$ long. See the detail drawing for their shape. Draw them on cardboard and then, with sharp scissors, cut them out.

The levers may bend a bit in the cutting process, but they will flatten out later on. Rub some glue on both sides of each lever to help stiffen them and keep them flat and even.

Place one piece of the quadrant on each side of the shift lever. You can fasten the quadrant pieces with two pins as shown, allowing it to separate about $\frac{3}{8}''$ as shown on the top view, or you can just glue the quadrant to each side of the hand lever.

The brake lever goes to the outside of the quadrant. It can be glued in place. If the quadrant is separated, run a pin through the bottom of the brake lever, through the bottom point of the outer quadrant piece, through the shift lever, and again into the point of the inner quadrant piece. Then cut off the pin. Either way, the quadrant is glued securely to the chassis side member just forward of the seats, as you can see by looking at the side-view plan.

Now take the steering wheel, see that it is free from excess glue and glue it to the end of the steering column. The steering wheel must be centered and at right angles to the steering column as well. See that it does not droop while drying. A bit of wood propped against it and the floorboards or cellophane tape will help to hold it in position while drying.

The wheels and the hub caps remain to be put on the car. Before you do that, paint the model. The body and chassis of the real car were white, as were the wheel spokes. The number 34 on the sides of the hood and the large gas tank were blue. In the model the tires are painted black. The steering column and the radiator shell are brass-colored. The steering-wheel spokes are aluminum or silver. Pedals and hand levers are brass-colored, as is the quadrant. Floorboard and firewall should be stained mahogany. The steering-wheel rim is brown. Filler caps for the tanks are brass-colored and the spare-tire wedge is brown.

If you draw on the louvers, they can be outlined with gray. If you put a strap over the hood, make it of paper cut in a strip ⅛″ wide and paint it brown.

The springs should be flat black. The instrument panel can also be painted flat black to bring out the white faces of the instruments, or it can be mahogany to match the firewall. The ¹⁄₁₆″-thick wood piece that goes alongside the motor hood is painted mahogany.

Of course, you may use your own colors, but in any event the tires should be painted black and the firewall and other pieces that are described as painted in mahogany should be so colored.

When the paint is dry, slip the wheels on the axles, the ones with brake drums going to the rear. Now make front hub caps by drilling about ³⁄₃₂″ into the center of a ³⁄₁₆″-diameter dowel that is cut off ⅛″. The ³⁄₃₂″ hole should be deep enough so that the hub cap fits over the end of the axle. Drill the ³⁄₃₂″-diameter hole into your dowel before you cut it off to length.

If you do not want to go to the trouble of making the wooden hub caps, you can use four brass washers ³⁄₁₆″ in diameter and drill the centers out if necessary to fit over the axle ends. Press the washers against the wheel hubs until the wheels turn around without wobbling on the axle. Then put enough glue on the axle and the washer to hold the washer securely in place. Make certain that you do not get any glue between the wheel and the washer, and make sure that the washer does not move away from the wheel while the glue is drying. If it does, the wheel will be too free on the axle and will wobble when it turns.

Of course, you can simply glue the wheels to the axle and not have them turn at all, but this is unlike a real car. In any event, make certain that all four wheels are touching the flat surface under them.

You can add two wheels or tires over the wood tire platform. These should be glued directly to the tire platform and the chassis. Paper tire straps, ⅛″ wide and painted brown, can be added, as shown on the side view. Cut the straps out of writing paper and glue them to the spare wheels. Your 1910 Bucket Seat Racing Car is now complete.

Chapter 10

Building the Cardboard Boat

It is possible to make a fine-looking model of an open-cockpit runabout that can be powered either by an inboard or an outboard engine. This kind of boat is found in most of the country's harbors, a popular craft for fishing and for family cruises on weekends and during the warmer months. In short, it is an all-around craft. Usually, these runabouts come in lengths up to 20 feet. The better ones are mahogany planked with teakwood decks and are powered by engines of well over 100 horsepower. Sometimes, instead of using an inboard engine, one or two very large outboards are hung at the stern. Either way, they are quite fast and very maneuverable.

Usually the top sides are painted white, with a black line at the water line, while the bottoms are painted bright red or green. However, the more expensive crafts have varnished mahogany top-sides, a gold line at the water line, and red, green or blue on the bottom.

Our model is a general composite of popular runabouts. Before you begin, you can obtain pictures of similar boats from the boating magazines and plan to adopt for your model the features that you like on them.

Although the model is of cardboard, it can be made to float and to contain an electric motor as well, making it a working model that will turn a fair clip of speed in the water.

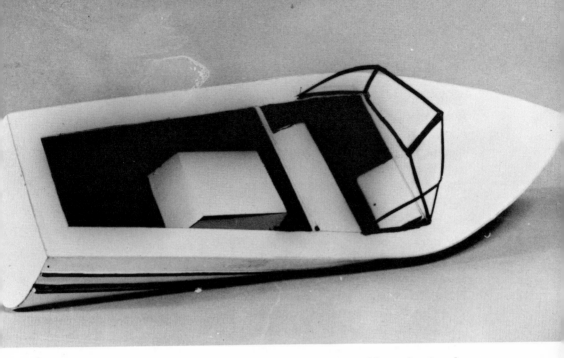

General view of the unfinished hull and interior of a cardboard boat showing the position of seats, dashboard, windshield, and engine cover. (*Kirt Miska*)

Study the plans first and read these instructions thoroughly.

It is essential that you use only quick-drying waterproof glue on this model. All holes or openings should be filled in with this cement wherever they might occur—pin holes, seams, spaces between the hull and the moldings, keel and hull, etc.

Use showcard or railroad board for the hull, deck, and cockpit, as well as for the three formers, or bulkheads. You might consider it better to replace the cardboard bulkheads with wooden ones on a working model. If you do, use something besides balsa wood. (While mentioning wood, the keel should be made of pine or bass wood because balsa wood is too soft for this part.)

The way the cardboard grain runs is just as important a factor in hull construction as it is in building model-airplane parts. Watch the way the arrows point on the plan, indicating the direction of the grain.

Trace out the pattern for the hull, carefully watching that you draw both sides, bow to stern, alike. Mark your center line as indicated by the CL letters. Then mark the position, also as indicated, where the center and forward bulkheads go. Note that there is a cut to be made along the center line of the bottom of the bow. Mark this off also.

Before you cut anything out, trace off the rest of the boat's patterns so that you will have this part of the work done. Since the bulkheads, forward and center, go into the hull after it is curved to shape, trace them out next. Then trace the stern piece. These items are made from either cardboard or wood $\frac{1}{16}''$ thick. If you make the bulk-heads of cardboard, make several of each and glue them on top of one another until the desired thickness has been arrived at. Use a heavy weight or several thick books to hold the laminated bulkheads together until the glue is dry. If the bulkheads are to be of wood, trace them out onto a $\frac{1}{16}''$-thick piece of pine or bass wood. Do not use balsa wood.

The two upper strips that go around the top outsides of the hull are drawn now, one for the left side and one for the right . . . in nautical language, "port" and "starboard."

The engine box covering, sides and top, should be traced next. Note that the grain of the cardboard runs across the motor cover.

The rear cockpit sills come next; then the rear cockpit sides, right and left, as marked in the drawings; after these, the front cockpit sides and then the rear cockpit piece.

The deck should be traced out carefully. Both sides of the deck must have the same curve. The pieces you cut out of the center of the deck later become the floor for the front and rear cockpit. Save them, of course, after you cut them out. The floor can be laminated for added strength to a $\frac{1}{16}''$ thickness. After you have drawn the deck, make your tracing of the windshield. Mark the center line where it is to be folded back at both sides.

Last of all, draw the keel on a piece of pine or bass wood $\frac{3}{16}''$ thick, about 17" long and about $1\frac{5}{8}''$ wide. The keel is wedge-shaped. The approximate position of the propeller placement is indicated on the plans. Since the propeller should be metal, it should be purchased. It is about 1" in diameter.

Now that you have drawn the parts on cardboard and wood, you have a pretty good idea of the various parts and where they go. Before you do any cutting, take a look at the exploded-parts drawing in order to see how they fit together. Using this as a guide, begin by cutting out the hull pattern with care, and see that you do not go off your marked lines. Do not bend or crack the cardboard in the process of cutting. Use clean, sharp scissors.

When the pattern has been cut out, very slowly curve the cardboard so that the sides of the hull come upward. Pinch the bow lightly until it closes and forms the sharp-pointed forward part of the hull. Hold the hull down on your flat work surface and gently work the sides up and inward with your fingers. Do this slowly and patiently to avoid cracking the cardboard.

The cardboard will form into the approximate shape you want. then separate the bow and put plenty of glue along the seam. Hold the bow together now with small pins inserted along it until it stays together of its own accord. Let it dry. Check it every once in a while. If it spreads apart, add a pin or two at that place. Do not worry about pin holes, for they can be filled in later on.

While the bow is drying, cut out the two bulkheads and the stern piece. Remember that they should be laminated or are made of wood $\frac{1}{16}$" thick. Each of these parts must be matched perfectly or you will have a lopsided hull when you insert them into it.

First place the forward bulkhead in position. It goes in place about $5\frac{3}{4}$" back from the top of the bow. Use plenty of cement and hold it securely to the hull sides with pins pushed through the sides into the edge of the bulkhead. Start with the bottom, lining up the center of the bulkhead with the center line of the hull. Put a pin in place at the center line and work upward with pins on each side until the bulkhead is fixed in position. The bulkhead's top and the top sides of the hull should touch. Allow the forward bulkhead to dry before inserting the center bulkhead.

The center bulkhead is put in place in the same manner. Allow the glue to dry. Now add the stern piece. This fits between the hull sides and is flush with the back of the hull. If you see that the back end of the hull does not match the stern piece exactly, do not worry. Allow the stern piece to dry in place first, held fast with pins. Then trim off any unevenness later on. Make certain that each bulkhead and the stern piece is exactly square across the hull. The top side of each bulkhead and of the stern piece must measure exactly the same distance back from the bow. The center bulkhead goes about 6" behind the forward bulkhead, and, of course, the stern piece fits at the rear of the hull, about $8\frac{3}{8}$" to the rear of the center bulkhead.

When all the inserted pieces have thoroughly dried in place, you can remove the pins. Be careful about this and see that you do not tear away any of the cardboard's surface that may have stuck to the pins because of the glue. Twist the pins around until they are free, before removing them. Sandpaper any excess glue away and then fill in all the pin holes. Rub the glue into them with your finger.

Next cut out the deck. Check both sides and make sure that they are the same. Your hull will not come out properly if you have more of a curve on one side than the other; nor will it sail correctly if you are making a working model. Be careful about your cuts when taking out the pieces for the cockpit openings. Use a good sharp X-acto blade in your holder and a steel ruler to guide you. Make several shallow cuts before you go all the way through the cardboard. Put aside the cut-out sections until later.

The deck is glued to the top side of the hull. It fits on top of the sides, not between them. The point of the deck's bow end lines up exactly with the hull's bow point and the stern is square with the end of the deck. Here, too, the center of the stern piece lines up with the center of the deck line. Do not be concerned about the rest of the deck. Use plenty of glue and fasten the deck to the hull sides. Hold it in place with pins until it is dry and then remove the pins. Fill in the pin holes with glue and fill in any space between the upper hull and the deck with model-car body putty.

The upper hull strips go on now, one on each side. Cut them out accurately so that they will match the hull sides properly.

Carefully pin the strips to the hull; the upper edge of the strips is level with the top of the deck. The bottom edge goes fast against the hull. You may have to twist the strips a bit in order to get these pieces to go on the way you want them to. Perhaps your cardboard will not form as it should and you may find that the rear part of the hull strips does not go exactly right. In case this happens, cut vertically through the two hull strips about 9¼" back from the bow. This will allow adjustments to be made along the deck line. If the bottom of the hull strips does not seem to have an even line, don't worry, for this will be taken care of later.

When the hull strips are fitted to your satisfaction, glue them in place as shown on the drawings. Use pins and plenty of glue to hold them in place. You may find it necessary to do your holding and gluing a little at a time in order to maintain the correct alignment. Allow the strips to dry, then remove the pins. Fill in the pin holes with glue. Next, take a strip of pine wood ⅛" square and run it along the bottom of the hull strips. Watch that the line of this length of wood is smooth and even. If it does not touch the hull strip in some places, leave it alone. Just make sure that the flow of the line of this strip is smooth. Glue it in place. When it has dried to the hull, fill in any spaces between it and the bottom of the hull strips with car body putty. Then sand smooth all over.

Although this ⅛"-square piece does not show in the exploded view, this molding and the strip below it at the stern, also of ⅛"-square pine, can be seen on the side elevation drawing. The lower rear ⅛"-square molding only goes forward 8" while the upper molding goes the full length of the hull. Glue the lower ⅛"-square molding to the hull 1¹⁄₁₆" below the upper molding.

Take the pieces that you cut out of the deck and place them inside the hull so that they line up with the cut-out portion of the deck. Cut out the two sides of the rear and forward cockpits. Mark them to make sure you put them in place correctly.

Insert the sides of the front cockpit first. See that they touch the cockpit floor at the bottom and line up with the deck at the top. If the floor is too low, then prop it up with a piece of ¹⁄₁₆" pine wood, as shown in the exploded view. Glue the floor in place first, and then the sides. Next add the forward wall. This piece is not given in the plans because you may want to leave the space open to receive batteries if the boat is to become a working model. However, it is a simple matter to cut a piece of cardboard to fit. Glue it in place and hold everything together with pins until dry. Remove the pins and fill in any holes or spaces with glue or car body putty.

The rear cockpit is built up the same way as the forward one, if the boat is not to be made a working model. The motor box or motor cover is cut out and glued to the floor and to a piece of laminated cardboard or wood $\frac{1}{16}''$ thick. This piece is inserted between the forward and the rear cockpits which it divides. It is capped with a flat piece of pine wood $\frac{1}{16}''$ thick and $\frac{1}{8}''$ wide.

Carve out the seat from a block of balsa wood to the size and shape given on the exploded view. Sandpaper it smooth and glue it in place. Next, add the dashboard to the forward wall. You can indicate the instruments on it before you glue it in position. Instruments can be black and the dashboard, or instrument panel, can be painted mahogany. A steering wheel may be fastened directly to the instrument board or mounted on a $\frac{3}{16}''$-diameter wood dowel which can be run through a hole made in the instrument board into another hole made in the forward wall, as shown in the side elevation. In either case, the diameter of the four-spoked steering wheel should be about $1\frac{1}{4}''$.

If you decide to make a working model, you have a choice of making the whole cockpit opening removable, or leaving the forward wall out for a compartment for batteries and having only the rear part of the cockpit removable.

Assuming that the rear of the cockpit is removable and you are going to place the electric motor there, the sides, bottom, front and back pieces of the cockpit should be glued together to form a box. The cockpit floor is cut away so that the electric motor will fit in and the motor cover actually covers it. The seat is glued to the floor of the forward cockpit, leaving the box-like rear cockpit free. All surfaces should be thoroughly shellacked.

The electric motor can be fastened to a pine-wood base, which in turn is glued to the hull sides or bottom. Angle the motor correctly so that the shaft will come out as is shown on the side-elevation drawing.

Since there is a good chance that the insides of the hull will become wet in the working model, spray or paint the inside of the hull and the bottom of the deck with five or six coats of waterproof paint or varnish. Get the paint or varnish into every crack and corner, and put it on thickly enough so that water cannot possibly get through it to the cardboard.

The keel, made of pine wood, is next to be put on the hull. Cut it out to the size and shape shown. Sandpaper it smooth. Then glue it to the bottom, exactly in the center of the outside of the hull. The rear of the keel should go about 2¾″ in from the stern piece.

However, if it is a working model, you will have to drill a hole through it for the propeller shaft. This must be angled so that it will meet the motor's shaft in a straight line. If you start the propeller shaft hole about ¼″ from the bottom of the keel at the rear, you have enough room to choose your angle. Keep in mind that you might have to double the thickness of the keel in order to put your shaft through without splitting the keel apart.

The propeller shaft is made in two pieces. The outer part of the shaft is a thin wall tube of brass, and the inner shaft, the one connected to the electric motor, can be either another brass tube or a brass rod. Generally speaking, the diameter of the outer tube can be about ⅛″. Using the telescoping tubing obtainable in model shops, you should have little or no trouble getting the correct size to insert into the ⅛″-diameter outer tube. The length to which you have to cut the tubes will depend on how and where you place the motor. The outer tube should be about 8″ long and the inner shaft or tubing about 1″ longer, leaving ½″ on one end to fasten the propeller to, and ½″ on the other end for the coupling to the motor. The inner shaft must rotate freely and it should have a little light oil covering its surface.

The center of the rudder post comes about ⅜″ forward of the stern, at the exact center line of the bottom. The post is made of brass if the model is a working model, and of dowel wood, if not. The post is 1″ long, having ½″ inserted into a hole in the hull and glued fast, if a shelf model. If it is to be a working model, use a brass tube with the top sealed watertight with solder, and insert it into the hull and glue it fast. Both the wood and the brass insert should be about 3⁄16″ in diameter.

With the wood dowel, you can use a cardboard rudder 1⅜″ high and 1½″ long. It is shaped as shown on the side-elevation drawing. If the model is to be a working one, then the rudder, made to these same dimensions, must be of brass and soldered to a 1½″ tube or rod. The end of the tube or rod is made to fit snugly into the brass rudder post. It must be fitted so it can be turned right or left without dropping out of the rudder post.

Whether the model is a working one or not, you will want to waterproof the outside so that moisture will not affect it. Therefore, the best thing to do is to give the entire hull at least three coats of clear lacquer spray or clear model enamel spray. Perhaps the best of all is four coats of white shellac, soaked into everything with a soft brush. Always allow each coat to dry thoroughly before putting on the next coat. If any roughness appears on the sprayed or painted surfaces, sandpaper it off with fine paper before applying the next coat. Wood alcohol is used for cleaning the shellac brush between coats, and lacquer thinner can

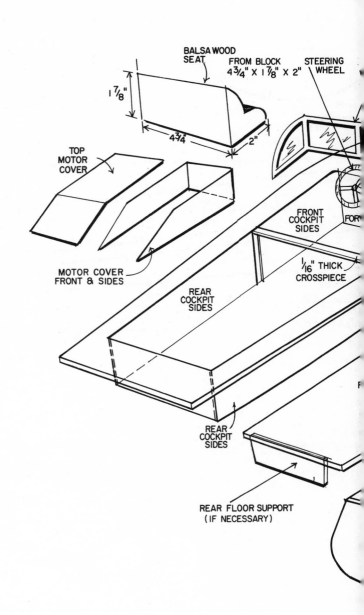

BALSA WOOD
SEAT
FROM BLOCK
$4\frac{3}{4}$" X $1\frac{7}{8}$" X 2"

STEERING
WHEEL

$1\frac{7}{8}$"

$4\frac{3}{4}$

2"

TOP
MOTOR
COVER

FRONT
COCKPIT
SIDES

FOR

$\frac{1}{16}$" THICK
CROSSPIECE

MOTOR COVER
FRONT & SIDES

REAR
COCKPIT
SIDES

REAR
COCKPIT
SIDES

REAR FLOOR SUPPORT
(IF NECESSARY)

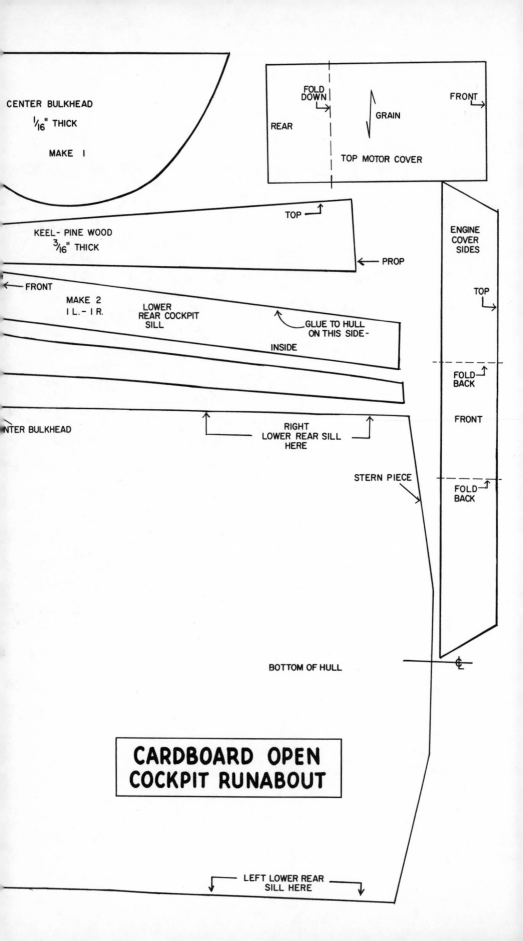

CENTER BULKHEAD

$\frac{1}{16}$" THICK

MAKE 1

FOLD
DOWN

REAR

GRAIN

FRONT

TOP MOTOR COVER

KEEL- PINE WOOD
$\frac{3}{16}$" THICK

TOP

PROP

← FRONT

MAKE 2
I L.- I R.

LOWER
REAR COCKPIT
SILL

GLUE TO HULL
ON THIS SIDE-

INSIDE

ENGINE
COVER
SIDES

TOP

FOLD
BACK

FRONT

NTER BULKHEAD

RIGHT
LOWER REAR SILL
HERE

STERN PIECE

FOLD
BACK

BOTTOM OF HULL

℄

CARDBOARD OPEN
COCKPIT RUNABOUT

LEFT LOWER REAR
SILL HERE

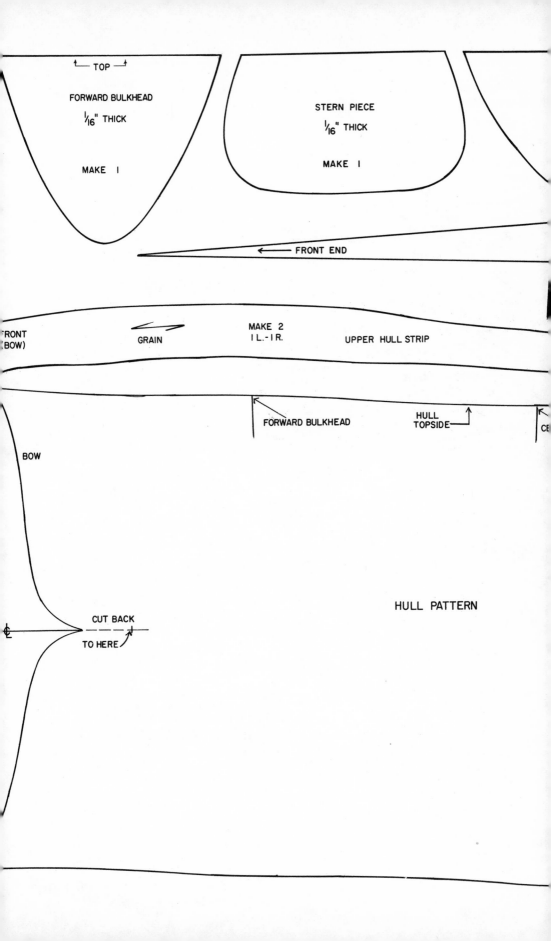

TOP

FORWARD BULKHEAD

1/16" THICK

MAKE 1

STERN PIECE

1/16" THICK

MAKE 1

← FRONT END

FRONT
(BOW)

GRAIN

MAKE 2
1 L.- 1 R.

UPPER HULL STRIP

FORWARD BULKHEAD

HULL
TOPSIDE

CE

BOW

CUT BACK

TO HERE

HULL PATTERN

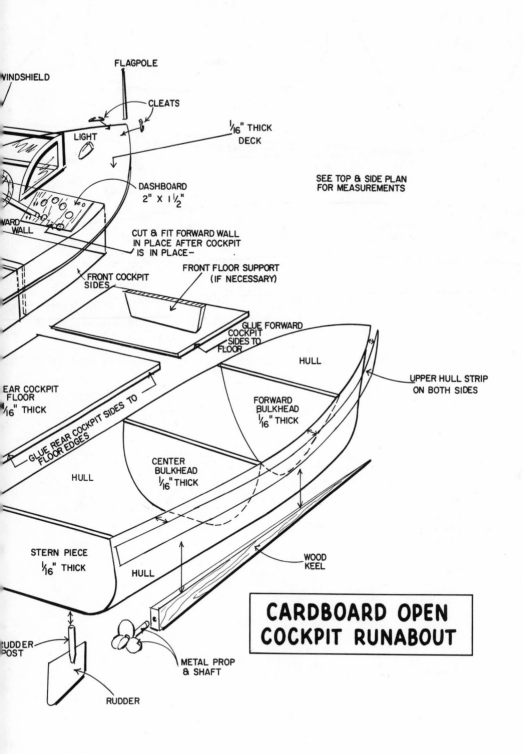

FLAGPOLE

WINDSHIELD

CLEATS

LIGHT

1/16" THICK DECK

DASHBOARD 2" X 1 1/2"

SEE TOP & SIDE PLAN FOR MEASUREMENTS

WARD WALL

CUT & FIT FORWARD WALL IN PLACE AFTER COCKPIT IS IN PLACE—

FRONT COCKPIT SIDES

FRONT FLOOR SUPPORT (IF NECESSARY)

GLUE FORWARD COCKPIT SIDES TO FLOOR

HULL

UPPER HULL STRIP ON BOTH SIDES

EAR COCKPIT FLOOR 1/16" THICK

GLUE REAR COCKPIT SIDES TO FLOOR EDGES

FORWARD BULKHEAD 1/16" THICK

CENTER BULKHEAD 1/16" THICK

HULL

STERN PIECE 1/16" THICK

HULL

WOOD KEEL

RUDDER POST

METAL PROP & SHAFT

RUDDER

CARDBOARD OPEN COCKPIT RUNABOUT

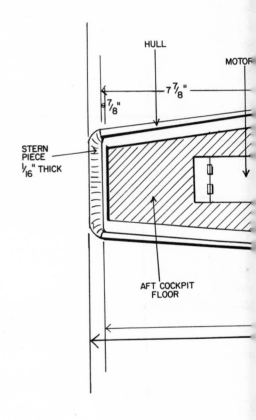

HULL

MOTOR

7 $\frac{7}{8}$ "

$\frac{7}{8}$ "

STERN
PIECE
$\frac{1}{16}$ " THICK

AFT COCKPIT
FLOOR

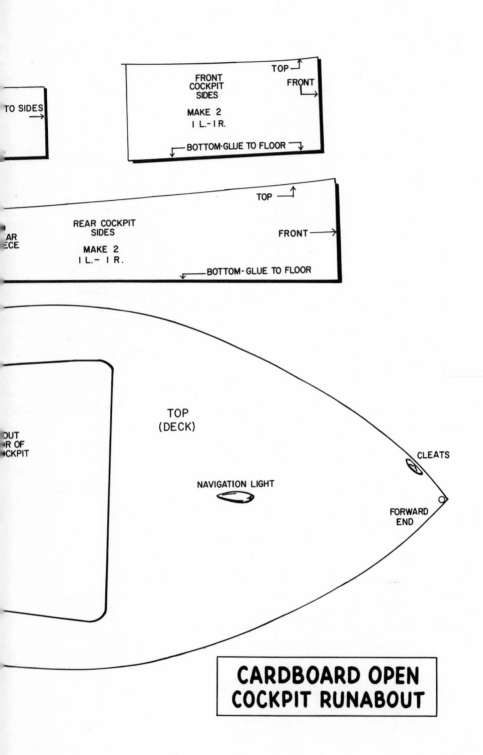

TO SIDES →

FRONT
COCKPIT
SIDES

MAKE 2
I L.- I R.

TOP →
FRONT →

— BOTTOM-GLUE TO FLOOR →

TOP →

REAR COCKPIT
SIDES

MAKE 2
I L.- I R.

AR
ECE

FRONT →

— BOTTOM- GLUE TO FLOOR

TOP
(DECK)

OUT
R OF
CKPIT

CLEATS

NAVIGATION LIGHT

FORWARD
END

CARDBOARD OPEN
COCKPIT RUNABOUT

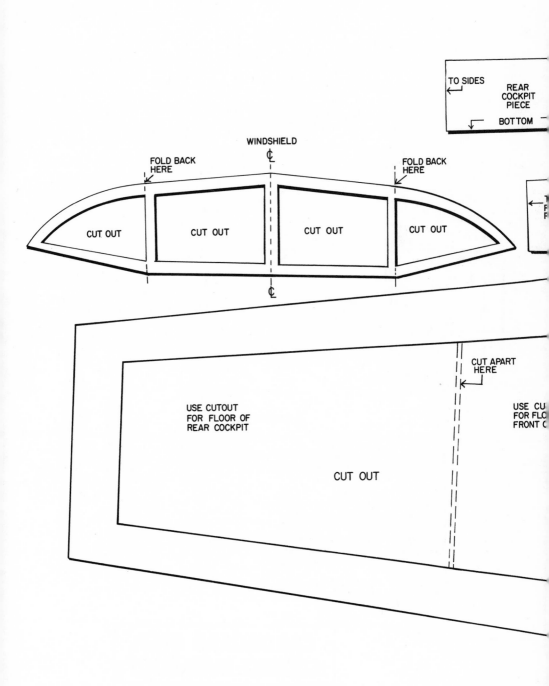

TO SIDES ←

REAR
COCKPIT
PIECE

↳ BOTTOM

WINDSHIELD

℄

FOLD BACK
HERE ↙

FOLD BACK
HERE ↙

CUT OUT

CUT OUT

CUT OUT

CUT OUT

℄

CUT APART
HERE

USE CUTOUT
FOR FLOOR OF
REAR COCKPIT

CUT OUT

USE CU
FOR FLO
FRONT C

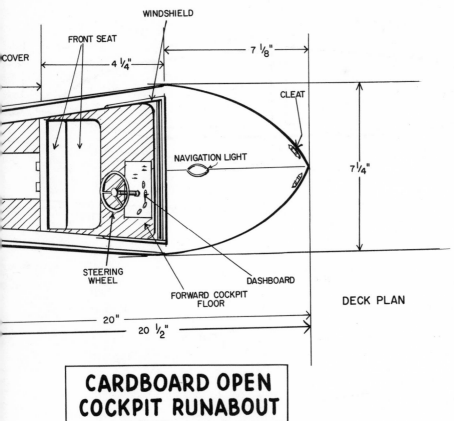

WINDSHIELD

FRONT SEAT

COVER

4 1/4"

7 1/8"

CLEAT

NAVIGATION LIGHT

7 1/4"

STEERING
WHEEL

DASHBOARD

FORWARD COCKPIT
FLOOR

DECK PLAN

20"

20 1/2"

CARDBOARD OPEN COCKPIT RUNABOUT

For remainder of Runabout plans,
see chapter 11.

be used to clean brushes if you decide to brush-paint the hull later on.

Painting the hull in its final coloring is easiest when it is done with a brush. In this case, at least three more coats of finish should be used. Paint color combinations is up to the builder, and something about this has already been mentioned. However, a good sandpapering between coats will help make a glossy surface if lacquer is used. Lacquer must not be used with anything else except lacquer. Shellac must have enamel or plain paint put over it. If you use a spray can, with paper and cellophane tape you must mask off the top sides while you spray the bottom of the hull up to the water line.

The windshield can be cut out while the hull paint is drying. It is shaped by bending the two ends back, leaving two openings at the front. Then it should be painted chrome, or mahogany, or the color of the deck. When dry, you may want to put transparent material into or over the cut-out openings. This should be glued in place with Elmer's glue. When complete, the windshield, in turn, is glued to the deck, just around the edge of the forward cockpit, with waterproof glue.

The two cleats that are shown on the top view, and the navigation light, are best purchased in a model store. They should be of metal. The cleats are ½″ long and the navigation light is about ⅞″ long and ¼″ wide. Also there is a flagpole at the bow which is made from ⅛″ dowel tapered toward the top. The pole should be about 1½″ high. You can also add a flagpole at the rear of the same diameter, but 2″ long. Place a navigation light, round in shape, on top of it; also two more cleats at the stern, if you wish.

The forward flagpole carries a pointed pennant in blue, red and white, or in any one of these colors alone. The rear pole carries the flag of the United States.

To make your model complete, the deck can be planked with $\frac{1}{32}$″-thick wood in $\frac{3}{16}$″ widths. This planking may be varnished, or painted a flat black first to indicate teakwood and then varnished, or it may be mahogany in actual wood or stained to look that way.

If your propeller is brass, it can be polished to a bright shine and have clear enamel sprayed over it to keep it glossy before it is put on the shaft. If the model is a shelf or display model and you have purchased a white metal propeller, it can be sprayed the color of the hull's bottom or painted to suit you.

Since the model must have something to rest on, make up a simple stand consisting of four wooden parts. For the base, use a flat board about 1 foot long and ⅛″ thick by 4″ wide. On this at either end fit a piece of flat wood ⅛″ thick, 2″ high and 4″ wide, carved out to take the shape of the bottom of the hull where these pieces will touch it. Then nail and glue them to the base. Between them add another piece of wood ⅛″ thick and about 1″ wide. Nail and glue this in place. Paint or stain the stand to your choice.

Chapter 11

The Cardboard Locomotive

Since we have a model of a cardboard airplane, a cardboard boat and cardboard automobiles, it seems right to include a cardboard locomotive. This serves to illustrate that cardboard, as a working material, is not limited to any one type of model, and that when it is handled carefully and properly, there is hardly any limit to its practical use for model making.

Most of the early locomotives were rather small, but by the year 1849 they had increased enough in size to make it necessary to add more wheels in order to carry the added length and weight of the boilers. Movable trucks and very large driving wheels also began to come into general use. Another improvement was the enclosed cab which took the place of open platforms on which engineer and firemen had stood, fully exposed to the weather.

One of the first locomotives to include these advancements was the Baldwin Single Driver of 1849. By today's standards, it was a queer-looking affair indeed. The two huge drivers poked their way up into the cab on either side and a pair of fixed wheels were placed just before them, while at the front sat a movable pilot truck with four small-spoke wheels. Between the small fixed wheels and the pilot truck were the cylinders. On top of the front of the boiler a very large funnel-shaped stack rose into the air.

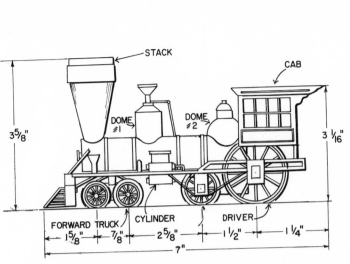

STACK

CAB

DOME #1

DOME #2

$3\frac{5}{8}$"

$3\frac{1}{16}$"

FORWARD TRUCK

CYLINDER

DRIVER

$1\frac{5}{8}$" $\frac{7}{8}$" $2\frac{5}{8}$" $1\frac{1}{2}$" $1\frac{1}{4}$"

7"

$1\frac{1}{4}$"

2"

PILOT WHEELS $\frac{5}{8}$" DIA.- SMALL WHEELS $\frac{13}{16}$" DIA.- DRIVERS $1\frac{5}{8}$" DIA.

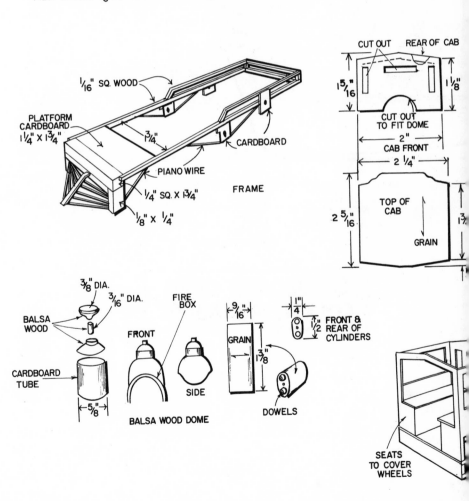

$\frac{1}{16}$" SQ. WOOD

PLATFORM
CARDBOARD
$1\frac{1}{4}$" X $1\frac{3}{4}$"

$\frac{3}{4}$"

CARDBOARD

PIANO WIRE

$\frac{1}{4}$" SQ. X $1\frac{3}{4}$"

FRAME

$\frac{1}{8}$" X $\frac{1}{4}$"

CUT OUT   REAR OF CAB

$1\frac{5}{16}$" $1\frac{1}{8}$"

CUT OUT
TO FIT DOME

2"

CAB FRONT

$2\frac{1}{4}$"

TOP OF
CAB

$2\frac{5}{16}$" $1\frac{3}{4}$"

GRAIN

$\frac{3}{8}$" DIA.

$\frac{3}{16}$" DIA.

FIRE
BOX

BALSA
WOOD

FRONT

CARDBOARD
TUBE

SIDE

$\frac{5}{8}$"

BALSA WOOD DOME

$\frac{9}{16}$"

GRAIN

$1\frac{7}{8}$"

$\frac{1}{4}$"

$\frac{1}{2}$" FRONT &
REAR OF
CYLINDERS

DOWELS

SEATS
TO COVER
WHEELS

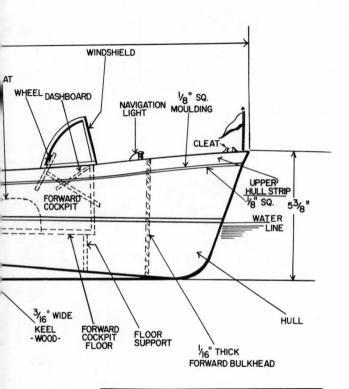

WINDSHIELD

AT

WHEEL DASHBOARD

NAVIGATION LIGHT

$\frac{1}{8}$" SQ. MOULDING

CLEAT

UPPER HULL STRIP $\frac{1}{8}$" SQ.

$5\frac{3}{8}$"

FORWARD COCKPIT

WATER LINE

HULL

$\frac{3}{16}$" WIDE KEEL -WOOD-

FORWARD COCKPIT FLOOR

FLOOR SUPPORT

$\frac{1}{16}$" THICK FORWARD BULKHEAD

CARDBOARD OPEN COCKPIT RUNABOUT

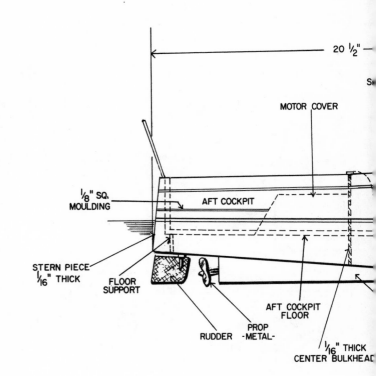

20 ½" —

S

MOTOR COVER

⅛" SQ.
MOULDING

AFT COCKPIT

STERN PIECE
1/16" THICK

FLOOR
SUPPORT

AFT COCKPIT
FLOOR

RUDDER   PROP
-METAL-

1/16" THICK
CENTER BULKHEAD

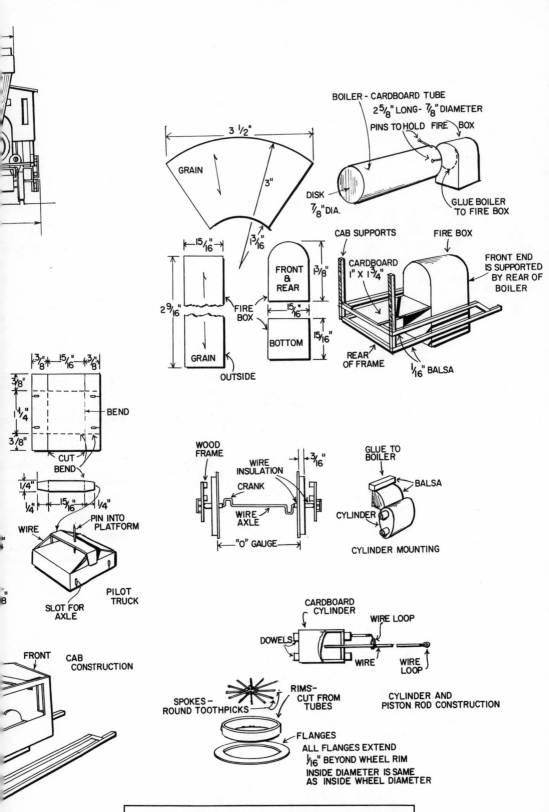

CARDBOARD LOCOMOTIVE

Both driving wheels were activated by connecting rods coming out of the cylinders and ending up on cranks cast into the axle of the driving wheels, rather than being fitted to the outside of the wheels as were the rods of most steam locomotives.

Probably because of their location, the drivers did not have enough weight placed on them so they had too little traction and, therefore, the engine could not haul a large load. This did not make them very useful and they were not successful. Actually, only four of them were built. Still, it must be said that they were fast, making a mile in 43 seconds. The last of them was constructed in 1851.

Because they were so rare and so very different from the usual run of steam locomotives, they are ideal for our model.

In order to make the model easy to construct, the O-gauge scale was chosen. It is assumed that a cardboard model of a locomotive would not be a working model but one for shelf or display purposes. However, if you wish, you can make the model of brass sheet, soldering where the cardboard-model parts would be glued together, and you can buy wheels instead of making them.

For those who want a model in the popular HO-gauge, the drawings and dimensions can be cut down. Choose your size and work accordingly. The instructions, which should be carefully read before starting the model, will be given for the larger O-gauge size model and will be kept as simple as possible, allowing you, who by now should have developed techniques of your own, to use them.

Begin with the frame. It is made of wood. Use pine or bass. Balsa wood is too soft for our purposes. Lay out the side pieces made of $\frac{1}{16}$"-square wood. Next add the two cardboard pieces that hold the axles of the small wheels and the drives. There are four—two to each side of the frame. Bend two lengths of piano wire to shape and fit them so that they go below the small wheels' axle supports and touch the frame as shown. Glue the wire securely in place. The wire should be about $\frac{1}{32}$" in diameter.

Next cut a flat piece of cardboard measuring $1\frac{3}{4}$" by $1\frac{1}{4}$" and fit it on the front of the frame so that you leave about $\frac{1}{16}$" of the front frame protruding. Glue it flush with the top of the $\frac{1}{16}$"-square side members. Add two $\frac{1}{16}$"-square pieces of wood between the side members at the rear of the frame, as shown on the plan. Glue everything securely together and allow to dry. Check to see that the frame is square and level. It must not have twists anywhere.

Cut three pieces of wood measuring $\frac{1}{8}$" by $\frac{1}{4}$". One piece is $1\frac{1}{4}$" long; the others, $\frac{9}{16}$" long. The longest piece is glued at the $\frac{1}{16}$" protruding front of the frame. The top is level with the top of the frame.

To each side of this $\frac{1}{8}$" by $\frac{1}{4}$" by $1\frac{1}{4}$" piece, at the bottom, glue

The underside of a cardboard O-gauge locomotive, showing the position of the front truck and drivers. (*Kirt Miska*)

a piece ⅛″ by ¼″ by 9/16″. These two pieces hold the cow catcher. Between them and below the 1¼″ length, glue a supporting piece of wood ⅛″ square. This piece is shown on the frame's perspective view, but it is not indicated.

Now you are ready to make up the cow catcher. This consists of five lengths of 1/32″-diameter piano wire bent to a shallow V and glued between the side supports, as shown. Space them about ⅛″ apart. See that they all have Vs of the same angle that get shorter as they go upward, as shown on the side view. Glue each securely in place and allow it to dry before putting in the next one.

Running up the center of the cow catcher's V is a piece of cardboard strip 3/16″ wide and 1″ long. Glue this in position after the wire pieces have securely dried in place. Note that it is bent toward the rear at its top.

A length of 1/32″-diameter wire is glued to the back of the cow-catcher support and the frame on each side. This wire piece is ⅜″ long and goes down the support about ¼″, where it is glued. The other end is glued to the frame. The side view will illustrate this.

The frame is finished now, except for the holes you must drill in the four cardboard axle supports. These holes are drilled in the axle support of the drivers 5/16″ from their top, not from the top of the frame.

The holes in the small wheels' cardboard axle support should be made $\frac{1}{16}''$ oblong so that the wheels can have a certain amount of up and down movement. These should be drilled about $\frac{3}{32}''$ up from the axle support's bottom. Axle diameter will depend on the diameter of the wire or wood dowel you choose to use, so drill your holes according to this. If you use heavy wire or a dowel larger than $\frac{1}{16}''$, you may have to make the supports somewhat longer than those shown on the plans.

Since it is much easier to fit the wheels into the frame before the boiler and cab are in position, the next parts to construct are the wheels. Before you do that, set up a length of track, either O- or HO-gauge, mounted on a thick board. This is used to keep the wheels to the correct spread or gauge, and helps keep everything level.

If you purchase the wheels, you can skip the instructions on how to make them, but mounting the wheels is about the same.

All eight of the wheels are made the same way, from cardboard tubes and wood toothpicks. Lay out, full size, a drawing of each of the wheels, on a smooth pine-wood board. Next, for the two large drivers, cut two rings $\frac{3}{16}''$ wide from a $1\frac{5}{8}''$-diameter cardboard tube. Put a piece of waxed paper over the drawing on the board and lay these rings over the drawing. Put pins all around the outside of the cardboard rim, holding it firmly and in place. It must measure the same from the center of the drawing to the inside of the rim at all points where the spokes will go.

Into the board, where the center is marked, drill a hole the diameter of the axle you are going to use. Drill about three-quarters into the board and make certain that the hole is vertical. Now place a length of your axle material, wood dowel or wire with waxed paper wrapped once around it, into the hole. Now you have the rim and you have the center point, the axle, in position. Neither rim nor axle should move.

The plan shows a main driver with 12 spokes. This was done to make the wheel simple, but you can add twice that many spokes if you wish to make the wheels to absolute scale. Any way you do it, the spokes must be the same distance apart and radiate outward at the same angle.

The spokes themselves are made of round wooden toothpicks cut off so that they fit snugly between the center axle and the inside of the rim. Cut one or two and fit them until you hit the proper length. Then test the correct one all around. Make up the rest of the spokes to match. Carefully, now, glue them in place to the rim and to each other where they touch at the hub, where the paper-covered axle is placed. The pointed ends of the toothpick spokes should be toward the hub.

111

Use enough glue to hold all spokes firmly in position and allow the glue to dry thoroughly. Then you can remove the wheel from the board. First take the pins away and then twist the axle stub at the wheel's center between your fingers. The wheel should spin around as you lift the axle stub out of its hole. The waxed paper under the wheel and on the axle stub should come away without any trouble.

Now you have a driver ready to mount a hub to, but before you do that, reinsert the pins over a new piece of waxed paper, insert another paper-wound stub axle and place the rim and spokes in position once more. Make your second driver in the same manner.

You will see that the drivers and all the wheels have a flange at their back. This flange should extend $\frac{1}{16}''$ beyond the rim on the four larger wheels and about $\frac{3}{32}''$ on the pilot wheels. To make this flange, work the same way for all the wheels. Lay the wheels (drivers first, because they are the ones we are making now) on a piece of cardboard large enough to circle the wheels with at least $\frac{3}{8}''$ of material left all around. Now trace the outside of the rims on the cardboard piece. Next mark between the spokes where the inside of the rim goes. Remove the wheel. Take a compass and find the center of the circles you just traced. Go over the circles once more with the compass and make another circle $\frac{1}{16}''$ outside them. You now have three circles. One matches the inside of the rim and one matches the outside of the wheel's rim. Then one more for the edge of the flange. Cut out the inner part of the circle first. Then glue the cardboard circle to the back of the wheel. The hole you have just cut out should match the inside edge of the rim. The middle circle should match the outside edge of the rim and will help you to center the flange. Glue the flange to the wheel securely. Allow the glue to dry and then cut off the cardboard exactly along the $\frac{1}{16}''$ outer circle. Now you have a wheel with its flange. Repeat the process on the other driver. Do not attempt to make the flange directly from the rim before you put the spokes in place. The cardboard rim has a tendency to be flexible and will not give you an exact circle. Make all flanges in the manner just described.

If you use a wooden axle, a dowel stick $\frac{1}{16}''$ in diameter, cut off the driver's axle about $1\frac{7}{8}''$ long. If you use wire and wish to make the driving rods work in and out of the cylinders, you will have to put a crank in each side of the axle just inside the wheels, as shown in the drawings. This will entail some modification in the width of the firebox and the diameter of cylinders themselves. You will have to work it out as you go along.

Since most builders will not use working parts, we will deal with plain wooden axles. The drivers are glued to the axles which are inserted into the hub ends of the wheel spokes. In order to do this precisely, place the drivers on the track. Allow the axle to extend at least $\frac{3}{16}$" beyond the outside of the rims of the drivers. Glue the axle to the wheels securely. In case the hub fit is a bit large, use paper wound over the axle as a shim to take up the space. Allow the unit to dry while mounted on the tracks, and make certain that they roll true and do not wobble. In other words, make them square to the axle both horizontally and vertically.

The axle for the small wheels just forward of the drivers should be of the same diameter as that of the drivers. This axle also should be of the same length, about $1\frac{7}{8}$", as the axle of the drivers. Flat wooden toothpicks are used instead of the round ones for the 12 spokes. The axles are fastened to wheels in the same manner. The flanges for the small wheels can be as wide as $\frac{1}{8}$" for a working model, as shown on the plans.

The pilot wheels, four of them, go beneath the forward part of the frame. These, constructed in the way we have described, also use flat toothpicks for spokes, of which there are 12. (You may use 8 or 10, if you wish to simplify matters.) If the model is to run, make the flanges $\frac{1}{8}$" wide as shown.

Unlike the other axles, those of the pilot wheels are of $\frac{1}{32}$" wire. When inserted into the hubs, the axle should extend only $\frac{1}{16}$" beyond the outside of the spokes. The axles themselves are about $1\frac{3}{16}$" long. Insert the axles into the wheels and glue them securely. Place the assembly on the track and check that the wheels roll correctly.

Next make the truck that holds the pilot wheels. This is a simple affair made of cardboard. The plans will give you the size and show you where and how to bend it. Actually it is a box, when folded to shape, that measures $\frac{15}{16}$" by $1\frac{1}{4}$". Glue it together and check to see that it is square and without a twist.

On top of the pilot truck is a length of cardboard $1\frac{1}{2}$" long by $\frac{1}{4}$" wide. The ends are bent down $\frac{1}{4}$" on each side as shown. Glue the ends to the outside of the truck so that each end goes down $\frac{1}{8}$" alongside the truck. Next glue four lengths of $\frac{1}{32}$"-diameter wire from the truck to the $\frac{1}{4}$"-wide piece that you have just put in place. When the glue has dried, cut out four oval holes for the axles. (The holes are oval in order to allow the pilot wheels to move up and down, providing a sort of spring and leveling action.) These four holes are spaced about $\frac{3}{16}$" in from the edges. Remember that the holes go in the $1\frac{1}{4}$"-long side. The holes themselves should be $\frac{1}{16}$" long and should come just about $\frac{3}{32}$" up from the bottom edge of the pilot truck.

In order to put the axles into these oblong holes, which should be no wider than $\frac{1}{16}$", cut a slit from the bottom of the truck up to the holes. Then slip the axles carefully into the oblong holes. The

113

axles and the wheel assembly should turn freely. Place the completed wheel and truck unit on the track. It should roll easily and evenly. If not, adjust it until everything works well. Add a drop of glue to the cut you made and see that it is closed up securely. Now find the exact center of the truck and run a long pin through it, as shown in the plans. Put the completed pilot aside until later.

Next insert the drivers into the frame. The frame will spread a bit, and so will the cardboard axle holders. Be sure you do not split anything while inserting the axle ends into the axle holders. The wheels should turn freely, but they will move from side to side until you wrap some cellophane tape around the axle or use wire insulation, as illustrated, between the spokes and the frame. This strip of tape should be just wide enough to maintain a clearance of $\frac{1}{8}''$ between the rims of the drivers and the inside of the frame. It can be less, though, if your rim is wider because of a different cut when making it. Wind tape or place insulation around the axle wide enough to hold the $\frac{1}{8}''$-clearance between rim and frame on each side.

Now insert the small wheels just ahead of the drivers. Check their movement and put cellophane tape or insulation around the axle between the wheels and the frame. Maintain the same clearance on each side.

Place the wheeled frame on the track and test it. It must roll well and it must point straight as it goes down the track. Adjust if necessary by removing the cardboard axle holders and regluing them. The journal boxes that go over the four axle holders are made of balsa wood, hollowed inside to clear the axle ends and glued in place.

Take the pilot and insert the pin into the cardboard piece at the front of the frame so that the flanges of the front wheels clear the back of the cow catcher by at least $\frac{3}{32}''$.

Place the frame, with all of the wheels in position, on the track once again. You may have to pull the pilot down in order to make the frame sit level. If so, glue a couple of small washers over the pin on top of the $\frac{1}{4}''$-wide cardboard until the correct distance has been obtained.

Now you are ready to construct the upper works. Begin with the boiler. It is made of a cardboard tube $2\frac{5}{8}''$ long and $\frac{7}{8}''$ in diameter. If a tube cannot be found, one can be made from a sheet of cardboard wrapped around a suitable wood dowel and glued together at the seam. Face off the front end with a cardboard disk.

Cut out a hole in the top of the boiler $\frac{9}{16}''$ in diameter and $\frac{1}{16}''$ back from the front for the stack to fit into. Then make the stack of cardboard. The pattern shape is given on the plan. Cut it out and glue it together at the seam. When the glue is dry, make a $\frac{3}{8}''$-wide band to go around the upper outside of the stack. Glue this band to

The front truck assembly ready to be placed in position under the front of the boiler. (*Kirt Miska*)

the stack, keeping the seam of the band and the seam of the stack in line. Once again allow the glue to dry and make a circle insert of cardboard from a piece $3\frac{1}{16}''$ long. This fits inside the stack, as is shown on the side and front elevations. About $\frac{1}{16}''$ of its width sits inside and the rest protrudes beyond the outer rim. Keep all the seams in line. When the glue has dried, insert the small end of the stack into the $\frac{9}{16}''$-diameter hole that you cut in the forward part of the boiler. The stack should stand $\frac{7}{8}''$ above the top line of the boiler. Glue it in place and make sure that it is exactly upright all around. Locomotive stacks never tilted to the right or left, or backward or forward.

In line with the stack and back from it $\frac{5}{8}''$ is dome number 1. Make it as shown on the plans. The bottom part, a tube $\frac{5}{8}''$ in diameter, is $9\frac{1}{16}''$ high. Carve the top fittings of balsa wood to the shapes shown. The lower part is about $\frac{1}{4}''$ thick while the dowel is about $\frac{5}{16}''$ long, with the upper part about $\frac{1}{4}''$ thick. Glue the sections to the top of the $\frac{5}{8}''$-diameter cardboard tube.

To mount it to the boiler, you can cut a hole $\frac{5}{8}''$ in diameter, in line with the stack, and insert the dome into this hole, $\frac{1}{16}''$ deep; or cut the bottom of the $\frac{5}{8}''$-diameter tube so that it is curved to fit the top of the boiler.

115

However you do it, glue it securely in position and see that it lines up with the stack and is vertical all around. Place a bent piece of $\frac{1}{32}$"-diameter wire to the rear of dome number 1, as shown in the side view. Simply glue it in position.

The firebox, which goes to the rear of the boiler, is $1\frac{5}{16}$" square and $1\frac{3}{8}$" high. The upper part is rounded. The shape of the bottom, front and rear of the firebox is given on the plan. Cut the pieces out, glue the front and rear to the bottom, and then place the $2\frac{9}{16}$" by $1\frac{5}{16}$" cardboard outside over the front and rear pieces. Note how the cardboard's grain must run so that you can curve the piece without cracking it. Glue all the parts securely. You can hold everything together with small pins until the glue has dried. Check that the fire box assembly is square and even all around.

Mount the firebox to the rear of the boiler. The top of the firebox and the top of the boiler should be on the same line. Center it so that the firebox extends downward in the same vertical line as the stack and dome extend upward. Hold the parts together with pins until the glue has dried.

Now add dome number 2 to the top of the firebox. This is carved out of balsa wood to the shape shown on the plan. The bottom of the dome is carved to fit like a saddle over the top of the firebox. The dome is about 1" high and about 1" in diameter. Glue it to the firebox after you have carved it out and sandpapered it smooth.

Take a piece of cardboard and cut out two $\frac{1}{2}$"-square pieces. Glue them beneath the boiler, just below the stack. Next add the cab floor, a cardboard piece indicated as 1" by $1\frac{3}{4}$", to the rear of the frame as shown on the plan. Now lay the boiler on the flat cardboard piece at the frame's forward end. It goes back $\frac{3}{4}$" from the extreme front of the frame. Place the cab floor against the firebox. Mark it where the rear of the frame ends and trim it off at that point. Fasten the boiler to the frame at the front by gluing the $\frac{1}{2}$"-square pieces that you have glued beneath the boiler to the flat cardboard piece of the frame. Then glue the cab floor to the back of the firebox and to the top rear of the frame. Be sure that the center line of the boiler–firebox combination and the cab floor is along the center line. The distance between the boiler and the frame must be the same on both sides, all along the length. Use pins to hold everything together until the glue has dried.

Make certain that the boiler is on the same horizontal line as the top of the frame. Place a piece of $\frac{1}{8}$"-square wood, the width of the cab floor, beneath the floor where it touches the firebox. This is for extra strength. Use ample glue here to make sure that everything holds well.

Assemble the cylinders next. These may be made of cardboard according to the plans, or you can make them out of hard balsa wood, carved and sandpapered to the shape and size given on the plan. If you use cardboard, you must cut out four end pieces. These are covered with a $\frac{9}{16}$" by $1\frac{3}{8}$" piece of cardboard which is wrapped over them. Everything is carefully held together with small pins until the glue is dry. Then the pins are removed and two $\frac{1}{8}$"-diameter dowel pieces $\frac{1}{8}$" wide are glued in place at the front ends of the cylinders.

If you plan to have working connecting rods, a hole $\frac{1}{16}$" in diameter must be made in the rear center of the cylinders to take $\frac{1}{16}$" wire which is used for connecting rods. The two connecting rods are fastened to the cranks on the axle by looping one end over the cranks and inserting the straight end into the cylinder. The straight end must be long enough so that when the crank turns the other end does not come out of the cylinder. Another piece of wire, looped and glued to the top of the rear of the cylinder, holds it in position, as shown.

The connecting rod operates in the same way if the cylinder is made of wood instead of cardboard. If the connecting rod is not working, it is simply glued to the rear of the cylinder and the other end which does not now need a loop is glued to a component near the axle of the driver.

Now place the cylinders below the number 1 dome and glue the cylinders to the inside of the frame. Add a piece of wood $1\frac{3}{8}$" square, with one end rounded, between the top of the cylinder and the side of the boiler. At the top of this rounded wooden piece add a length of wood $\frac{1}{16}$" square by $\frac{5}{8}$" long. Glue this in place as shown. Put the connecting rods in place.

Just about halfway down the side of the boiler and in line with the stack, place two cardboard braces, one on each side. Fit them between the outside top of the frame and the boiler where they touch. Shape them as shown and glue them firmly in position. Add two more braces, this time made of $\frac{1}{32}$"-diameter wire, to the front of the frame and to the boiler. Only one more pair of braces remains to be fixed to the frame and to the boiler. They go in front of the cylinders. These are made of $\frac{1}{8}$" wood dowel and are cut off so that they fit between the boiler and the inside of the frame. Glue them in position.

Make the cab next. It is built of four pieces of cardboard, cut out as shown on the plan—a front, two sides, and a top. Take the pattern shape for the sides from the side-elevation drawing. The measurements for the side pieces are $1\frac{1}{4}$" high by $1\frac{3}{8}$" wide at the bottom. The sides are $1\frac{3}{4}$" wide where they are scalloped and touch the roof. The windows in the sides are ⅝" high and 1" long. The top of the windows is ³⁄₁₆" below the top line of the sides. If you wish to insert the grill in the window opening, make it of ¹⁄₃₂" wire, cut to fit. There are three uprights and one cross-piece. These should be glued in position before the sides are glued to the cab front.

The cab front is 1⁵⁄₁₆" high at the center peak, 1⅛" high where the sides are glued to it, and 2" wide. Three windows are cut out of the front piece; one is 1" by ¼" at the top center, and two are ¾" by ³⁄₁₆" at the sides, as you can see by looking at the plans.

The top, or roof, is 2¼" wide and 2⁵⁄₁₆" long. The shape is somewhat irregular at the rear while the front of the top is simply slanted backward ⅛" toward the outer ends.

Glue the sides to the front pieces. Put them together squarely. The top corners of all three pieces must touch accurately, but you will note that the bottom of the sides will go lower than the bottom of the front piece.

Next glue the unit back of the dome of the fire box. The bottom of the cab sides should be ⅜" above the top members at the rear of the frame. Add two ¹⁄₁₆"-square uprights at the corners, as shown, to support the rear of the cab, and glue these securely to both the top rear of the corners of the frame and the insides of the cab. However, in place of these uprights, you can use a cardboard cut-out made to the shape shown in the cab's rear perspective view.

In either case, two seats are fitted inside the cab. These are made of cardboard pieces glued in position. The upright pieces should measure about ⅝" high and 1⅜" long, and be glued to the cab floor, one on each side. Then they are braced with two other cardboard pieces at their tops, measuring 1⅜" long by ⁷⁄₁₆" wide. These form the cab seats. You might find it necessary to adjust these sizes because of the particular kind and thickness of cardboard you use.

If you have put a cardboard cut-out at the rear of the cab, then the cab is complete except for adding the top. But if you use the wood uprights, then cut out two small pieces of cardboard about 1¹⁄₁₆" by ⅝". Trim them to fit and glue them to the rear of the seats. You may need a rear platform back of the seats, and this can be made of cardboard also. Fit it on top of the rear of the frame. The back of the frame itself is finished off with a cardboard piece about ⅜" wide and 1⅞" long. Glue it in place.

Next cut out and glue the top to the cab. Fit it so that the front corners line up with the front top corners of the sides, but allow an overhang at the front and the rear, as shown on the drawings. You will also see that there is about ⅛" overhang of the top on the right and the left sides. Hold the top in position with small pins until the glue has dried. This completes the construction of the model.

The completed model with tender represents hours of interesting work and resultant satisfaction. (*Kirt Miska*)

Any other detail the builder wishes to add can be found on the plans and in photographs.

Remove any pins that you may have left in place. Fill in all pin holes with model-car body putty as well as any cracks or unwanted openings. Allow the putty to dry and then carefully sandpaper it smooth. Do not rough up the cardboard when sandpapering.

Now you are ready to paint the model. First of all, see that everything is smooth. If you have any roughness left from the sandpapering itself, rub quick-drying glue over it until it smooths out. Give the entire locomotive a spray of clear enamel, the kind used for models. Do not gum up the wheels and axles with the spray so that they cannot turn. Allow the spray to dry and cover the model with a box to prevent dust from settling on it.

If you do not want to use spray, you can brush on a thin coat of white shellac, although this will take longer to dry.

Colors for the Baldwin Single Driver Locomotive Model are black, green and red. Black is used for the frame and front of the boiler, the stack, the tops of the wheel-rims and their flanges, the pilot truck cow catcher and the top piece of number 1 dome. Green is used on the rest of the model except for the outside of the rims and the grill of the cab windows, which are bright red. The covers of the journal boxes also may be red.

A name or number may be inscribed on the sides of the cab below the windows. You may wish to add the four brass bands around

119

the boiler. Two go before the number 1 dome and two after it. They are about ⅛″ wide and are made of brass-finished, metal, stripping tape which is obtainable in model shops. The other brass bands go around the upper parts of both domes. Do not put the brass bands on the locomotive until all the paint has dried.

If you want to make a tender for the model, you will have to make four wheels about the size of the pilot wheels. These are placed on wire axles just as you did before. Then a frame is made of cardboard ¼″ wide. The sides measure 2½″ long and the front and rear measure 1⅝″ wide. Make axle holders like the ones on the locomotive, although you can use your own design. These are placed outside the frame and the axles are inserted into them in the same way as you did for the drivers.

Next fit a square cardboard box on top of the frame. It should be about 2⅛″ long, 1½″ wide and 1¼″ high. Push the bottom of the box, a flat cardboard piece made to fit inside, up from the bottom ¼″ to clear the wheels.

A frame of cardboard strips ⅛″ wide can be placed around the edges of the box for decoration. The inside can be filled with bits of twigs glued in place to represent firewood. Make a hook of 1/32″-diameter wire and glue it to one end of the finished tender. This hook should be U-shaped. One end of the U is glued to the tender while the other is the hook to the back of the locomotive. This fits under the rear of the locomotive's frame. The pictures will give you some idea of the type of tender you can build. Paint it the same way as you did the locomotive in matching colors.

Remember to work carefully. Never hurry, for most of the fun of model making is in the actual making of it.

Chapter 12

Plastic Kits, Detailing Plastic Models and Collector's Items

Now that you have read the preceding chapters and have built the models, you have enough experience to take on the construction of kits of cars, boats and airplanes made of plastic and other materials.

In some cases, the plastic model kits will be found to be a very quick and easy job of assembly, especially when you choose the newest Revival Kits made by Renwal. Others will present more problems, for they are complicated because of the realism of their construction and because of the numerous small parts that go to make up a single unit.

Two examples of plastic kit engine construction are illustrated by the accompanying drawings taken from the instruction sheets of the Jo-Han Turbo Car, showing the most modern advancement in engines for automobiles, and the Jo-Han Cadillac V-16 of 1931 vintage. By studying these two drawings, you can gain an excellent idea not only of the type and number of parts used, but also of how they are arranged and go together. These models are built to $\frac{1}{25}$ scale.

You will see that there is a sequence to the assembly and the kit model maker must adhere to this sequence, especially if he is "new to the game."

Also illustrated are two engines of modern sports cars made from the plastic kits for the Jaguar XKE and the Chevy Corvette.

Renwal plastic antique aeroplane model kits are inexpensive to buy and easy to put together. This company makes a wide variety of kits.

These are Monogram models and are ⅛ the size of the actual car. They will give you an excellent idea of the super-detailing that can be found in kits. This kind of model can be yours with patience, careful study of the kit instructions, and enthusiasm for doing good work.

A book about models and model making would never be complete if some mention were not made of the metal-plastic models that are imported into the United States by such firms as Schuco in New York City. Schuco also makes a wonderful line of spring-driven metal toys, or models, about 8″ long that are beautifully detailed and accurate. Two of them are outstanding, the Mercedes-Simplex of 1902 and the antique Maxwell Roadster. Also made in the same scale by Schuco are the Mercer 1913 and a Ford Coupé.

The Mercedes is a wonderful thing. It can be left as purchased, or you can add details to make it uniquely your own. Such details might include leather covering on the seats, carpet (fabric) on the rear floor, scored aluminum covering for the front floorboards, dials on the dashboard, fasteners for the motor hood and the painting of the steering wheel in brown-mahogany. In either case, this is a remarkable miniature.

Of a smaller size, mostly 4½″ long, are the Italian-made Dugu models. These are built to ⅟₄₃ scale. They are beautifully detailed cars and are a combination of plastic and metal construction. The Fiat 1907 Racing Car, for example, has a chain drive that really works, while the Itala 1912 is super-detailed with everything on it including a "snake horn." The Lancia Lambda of 1925 is an exact model of one of the most advanced automobiles ever created.

From France come even more beautiful models made by Solido. They offer a series of fabulous automobiles—Mercedes SS of 1928, Panhard-Levassor of 1925, Voisin of 1934, Hispano-Suiza of 1925, and the magnificent Bugatti Royale of 1930. If you take a good look at the illustrations of the Panhard and the Voisin, you can readily see just how truly wonderful these ⅟₄₃ scale super-models are, especially when you realize they are only 4″ to 5½″ in size.

These, like the Dugu models, are just about perfect for the accomplished model maker to work on. Being so excellent, they prac-

With kits from Renwal you can make your own fleet of crazy flying machines.

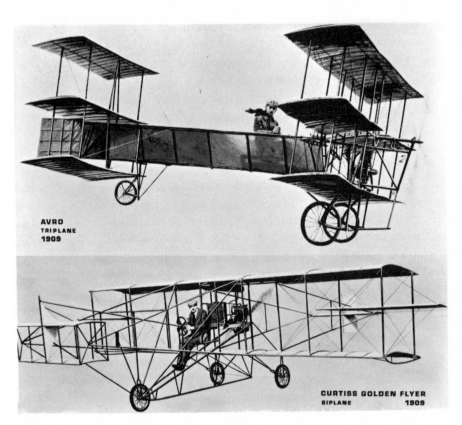

AVRO
TRIPLANE
1909

CURTISS GOLDEN FLYER
BIPLANE   1909

123

tically ask for extra touches such as striping, spotlights, custom painting to bring out molding lines, leather-covered seats, bumpers, chrome coloring of the door handles, filler caps, hinges and contrasting colors for the wheels. Then if you are really excited about this type of work, you can also add the brake drums on some of them as well as scale front axles and even repaint the models to suit yourself.

However, you should make certain that you have many photos of the real machines together with close-up pictures of their various parts, before you attempt this kind of work on models of such high character.

Last but not least are the Hispano-Suiza models made by EKO in Spain. While they are not of as high a quality as the Dugu and Solido miniatures, the EKO models lend themselves to a good amount of detailing which, when correctly done, will produce as fine a model as you can hope to get. Things like rugs on the floors, striping, repainting, rebuilding of the chassis parts, repositioning and adding spokes to the wheels and dials to the dashboards are just a few of the additions that the progressive collector and modeler will find interesting to make. Three styles of Hispano-Suiza cars are available—the Touring, the Limousine, and the Alfonso XIII Sport Roadster.

Cardboard models need not be made from scratch. Many Schreiber models are ready to be cut out and assembled and can be made by a model maker who may or may not have a lot of experience. If you can use a scissors, spread on glue and fold, you can have a fine-looking cardboard model, using these kits.

The difference between experience and lack of it will show up in the neatness of construction and the builder's ability and desire to add details that the cut-outs do not have, such as rubber tires, interiors, and windows that are made to see through. The more experienced builder can, after working on the Panel Truck and Bucket Seat Racing Car, rework the chassis of car models like those in the Schreiber series so that he will have a more accurate model.

Included in the Schreiber cardboard cut-out line are models of ocean liners and aircraft carriers almost 5 feet long. In spite of their being made of cardboard, these ship models can be made to float and are extremely strong when completed; indeed, somewhat better than many balsa-wood models.

If you look carefully at the illustrations, you can see for yourself just how good the bought cardboard cut-out models are.

In the next paragraphs are suggestions and some methods for the detailing and improving of models, either home-made or built from kits. The description for detailing will deal mainly with automobiles, but much the same ideas can be used for other kinds of models, whether they are boats, airplanes, or locomotives.

This cardboard model of the 1909 Baker Electric actually works—the top folds and the wheels steer. (*Kirt Miska*)

If you cover the seat of a model car or a speedboat in leather, it is cut out to fit and put on with glue.

Extra details on cars, boats and locomotives, such as lights of one sort or another, differ only in design, but they are mounted with either glue or solder and all are either polished or painted.

Aircraft seats, like those of boats and automobiles, are covered with leather. Dashboards or instrument panels of airplanes and cars are so alike that any description of either can be used for both.

Ship model rigging is usually a process of tying and gluing thread from one mast, or spar, to another. Rigging airplanes is a matter of tying and gluing thread from one strut to another. If you know how to do one, you know how to do the other.

Painting models, as mentioned before and can well be mentioned again, is a matter of care and patience. Parts are usually painted before assembly in order to make things easy and to prevent slopping unwanted color onto an already painted surface. Good brushes, always kept clean, are a "must."

Good color selections and combinations are a most important consideration when detailing models.

To give you an idea of color and how it should be used to make a model more detailed and therefore more accurate, let us assume that you have finished a racing car model. Now you want

A Bentley in the process of becoming a detailed scale model. (*Kirt Miska*)

The British-made Bentley plastic model as a track racer. (*Kirt Miska*)

to color it and you imagine that the color green would be just the thing for the car. Perhaps bright gold wheels would look good, too. Maybe the seats should be orange and the bottom yellow. Of course, this would be a very bright model, but it would also be wrong.

First, the color green was never used on racing cars that competed in national events in the United States. Green was considered a bad-luck color by drivers, who would not drive cars so painted.

Second, gold wheels. Circus wagons had them, and sometimes the royal coaches of kings, but gold is not correct for racing cars.

Third, leather for seats in the early 1900's came in such colors as black, brown, natural, red or green. To get orange leather, a brush and paint would have to have been used over the original color. It is highly unlikely that anything was used on the leather except saddle soap and a special oil to keep it soft and clean.

Fourth, since the bottom of the racing cars was usually the same color as its top sides, the only other color used was black. Painting the bottom of an antique racing car a different color from what it was originally spoils its looks, and is the sign of an inexpert and unknowing builder. It is important to choose the right coloring.

Now, of course, the question comes up, "How do I know what the right color is?" Well, first of all, never try to make a circus wagon out of any model. Never try to make a ship model look like a hot dog stand, all yellow and black! Don't dream up wild colors for

The Mercedes-Benz 500K roadster just as it comes from the Jo-Han kit.
(*Kirt Miska*)

The front view of this Hubley metal Packard touring car would fool anyone into thinking it the real thing. (*Edelstein*)

steam locomotives. Steam engines were usually black, with some striping added occasionally, in gold, green or deep red. Some of the early locomotives were green and red. Some European locomotives were combinations of black and green with reddish parts or striping.

Paintings of ships will almost always give you an excellent idea of how they were colored. These paintings can be found in museums. If you can't get to a museum, there are books about ships in the public libraries that have color prints. Calendars from shipping companies have colored pictures or paintings of vessels of many types on them. Your colors can be copied from these. You can even write to the ship-building companies and explain to them that you are making a model and want something to give you the correct colors for your model of their particular ship or boat. Usually if you build from a kit, the correct colors are given in the instructions.

Since scale locomotives are very popular, you can go to almost any model shop that has a display of locomotive models and see for yourself just how they are painted. The man at the model store will be glad to help you pick the proper color and the right kind of paint.

Model airplanes are a bit easier. The covers of many model-airplane and model-making magazines have pictures of all kinds of air-

A cardboard model of the 1925 Locomobile, built to scale by the author. The doors and the windshield are movable. (*Kirt Miska*)

craft. Usually the model kits have fine color pictures of the real airplane in detail on the box they come in.

Automobile models, especially of the antique, vintage and classic cars, should have the correct colors. Quite naturally, someone will

The Cadillac V-16 touring car of 1931 as built from a Jo-Han kit. (*Kirt Miska*)

The Hubley metal model chassis of a customized Packard. (*Kirt Miska*)

ask, "If the cars could be painted to suit the purchaser at the factory, before they were delivered, why can't I paint my car model any color I want?" Some of the reasons were explained earlier. Of course, you can paint your model as you like, but if accuracy is important to you, a little research is often necessary. Check your library or book store for pictures of old cars; examine old catalogs and magazines for color pictures or descriptions. In some cases, the automobile company will tell you the proper color for your car model if it is still in business.

A Cadillac V-16 chassis from a Jo-Han plastic kit. (*Kirt Miska*)

This 500K Mercedes chassis from a Jo-Han kit features finely detailed wire wheels.
(*Kirt Miska*)

Car model-making magazines, too, like most model magazines, have color covers picturing cars, and many companies put out calendars with colored pictures and photos of the old cars on them. You can always get in touch with one of the many antique automobile clubs and they will help you. Also go to the old car meets during the summer months and see the old cars for yourself. There is much to learn just by looking and asking questions.

The metal chassis of the Hubley Duesenberg before installation of the engine.
(*Kirt Miska*)

The Hubley Duesenberg with engine, steering and drive train in place. Assembly is done with screws and screwdriver. (*Kirt Miska*)

The best way to find out about other details, aside from the proper color, is to try to get a look at the real thing. This is true about any model you make, whether it be car, boat, ship, plane or locomotive. Take a camera with you and take close-up photos of the details you want to include in your model, and as many other photos of the whole thing, from as many angles as you can. A good photo is extremely valuable as a source of information about details.

Pictures wherever you find them are useful in pinpointing details that you may want to put on your model. The photos in the car catalogs may show you exactly where the steering arm is placed and where a hinge or handle actually goes.

A picture of a ship or boat will give you an idea of where a searchlight should be and how the rigging is set; or how and where the flags are placed.

The aircraft pictures will also give you the correct numbers and letters that go on your model as well as the control wire positions or the squadron insigne and engine details.

Locomotive pictures will usually show you what kind of trains your locomotive was used to pull; where the rivets, piping and steam domes were placed; how various locomotives of the same type, but used by different railroads, were equipped. You can spot the different kinds of reversing gear, cow catchers or stack sizes.

It is helpful to have pictures of the model you are making always before you, especially when you want to detail the model beyond anything a kit or its instructions give you. A good magnifying glass is a big help in searching out indistinct details or making sure of the clear ones in your photos.

Once you have figured out about what you want to do in order to make your model a better one, look around for parts that will suit the model. Special car lights, wheels or fenders; anchors, vents, lifeboats, wheels and capstans on ships and boats; correct size wheels, machine guns, markings and instrument boards on airplanes; whistles, lamps, piping, and decals on locomotives.

Usually you can get the parts you need for the locomotive, modern airplane, ship or boat model that you are making at almost any good model shop, and in the scale you want. These models seldom present any problem.

Finding a certain scale rotary or radial engine or the proper size wheels for older airplanes can be quite another matter. Your best bet would be to try to make them yourself. This can be done by using the chapter about the construction of the Waco Biplane as your guide. Sometimes, though, you will find a part in one plastic kit that will fit your need for a model being built from a different kit. Use it.

The twin overhead camshaft engine of the Hubley Duesenberg, showing the wealth of fine detail. (*Kirt Miska*)

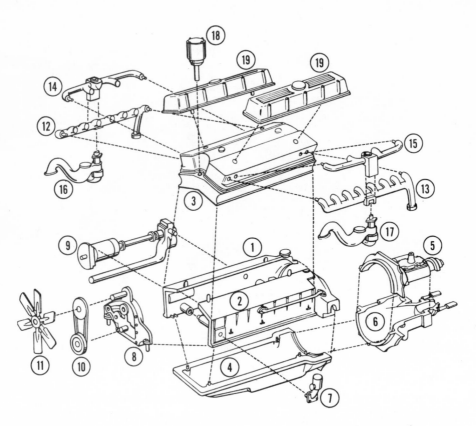

This exploded view of the 1931 Cadillac engine comes with directions for assembling in the Jo-Han kit.

Car models, especially of the old timers, which are the most popular at the moment, pose something of a problem with respect to interchanging parts. No model-making company has as yet a line of extra parts one or more of which you can purchase to put on a model of an old vintage car.

Sometimes the modern dragsters have wire wheels that you can adapt to fit your old-car model; or a front axle that can be used. Some of the chrome headlights found in late-model hot-rod kits can be of use.

The springs from one model may fit another chassis; and by adapting these springs, a lower and more proper "sit" for your model can be obtained. The use of the right springs, particularly at the front of an old car chassis, is often a necessity. The kit front axle might not be in the correct position when you check it against your photos or a tie rod might not clear the bottom of the radiator. Proper springs will help.

You may want to use spoke wheels or disks, or wire wheels of a different design from those you receive with the kit. Your photos

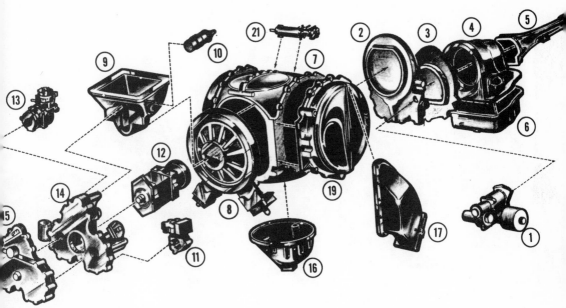

The exploded view of the engine of a turbo-car from a Jo-Han kit shows the relationship of parts to each other.

may have shown you the difference. You should look in a different kit first for the wheels you want. You can cut down the spokes of wood-type wheels found in other kits and glue them into the rims from the kit you are building, for one thing. Then again you may want disk wheels. You can cover the spokes that are in the wheels you have, front and back, with disks of cardboard, painted properly, or made of aluminum and polished.

Many times the wire wheels do not have the correct number of spokes in them; or the spokes are much too heavy. This is a difficult problem to lick. Since wire wheels are always the most important part of the model they are on, care should be taken to see that they are correct.

You can add extra spokes to the wheels by cutting off short lengths of piano wire and gluing them into the wheels between the plastic spokes, until the number of spokes looks right. The experienced model maker can take out the plastic spokes and add all wire ones, but this is a long and difficult job. An entire chapter can be written about making wire wheels, but since we are only concerned with suggesting how to detail your model, we must leave out lengthy instructions concerning any one part.

Any number of combinations of fenders can be used. A good idea of what can be done will be gained by looking at the photo of the Lincoln Holbrook Cabriolet. This model used the Lincoln chassis

The Stutz Bearcat of 1923 made of brass from scratch on a scale of ¾ inch to 1 foot. Springs and shackles, steering, top and windshield all work. (*Kirt Miska*)

This Stutz Bearcat is a combination of scratch-built and kit-built. "Scratch-built" means that parts are made by the builder. In this case, the kit parts were also re-worked by the builder. (*Kirt Miska*)

A large working model of a 1911 Mercer was re-built into this detailed raceabout.
Seats are leather, floorboards are aluminum foil. (*Kirt Miska*)

Metal models of the Voisin Sedan (*left*) and the famous Bugatti Royale are made
in France by Solido. (*Kirt Miska*)

An exploded view of the Voisin 1934 Carene by Solido illustrating the parts, all made to a scale of 1 to 43. (*Kirt Miska*)

and front fenders. The running board and rear fenders were taken from a Cadillac kit. You will notice that the combination works out extremely well. The same thing can be done on other models by using fenders from a model A or T Ford or a Chevrolet. Cardboard skirts and rear fender wheel enclosures also may be glued to the fenders in order to copy the lines of the cars of the late thirties.

Sometimes the cycle-type fenders found in hot-rod and dragster kits can be used on sport and sport-racing cars of the 1920's and 1930's. It is also possible to remove the fender wells that the side-mounted wheels fit into and fill in the openings with cardboard backed up and filled in with model-car putty, if, for instance, a long, sweeping fender is needed.

From left to right, small-scale Italian models of the Fiat Racer, the Lancia Lambda, and the Itala Touring Car. (*Kirt Miska*)

Various combinations and changes of bodies from one chassis to another are also possible if you wish to make a detailed model of a particular car and there is no kit for that car.

Using the Lincoln Cabriolet again as an example—and you can see that this is not a kit offering—the body was built up using two other kit body parts, a back end and two sides. These, when cut to shape and filled in with body putty, made an exact duplicate of the

A metal working model of the 1902 Mercedes by Schuco that is really a toy but comes close to being a scale model. (*Kirt Miska*)

The early Vauxhall Roadster, made of cardboard from a cut-out scale model layout by Schreiber. (*Kirt Miska*)

style wanted. A leather top was added to the plastic sides together with metal molding.

Other details on this particular model will give you a further example of how completely this kind of interchange of parts can be used to build and scale-detail a plastic kit model.

The headlights were made from running board searchlights of a different model. The Lincoln kit headlights were not proper for the year of the Holbrook Cabriolet, so they had to be changed. The front axle was also moved slightly forward to take away the "nosed-over" look of the kit, just to indicate another small detail. A new top for the motor hood was also fashioned from the top piece of yet another kit, to obtain a better fit and line between the Lincoln radiator and the cowl. The Landau irons, on either side of the leather top behind the windows, were taken from the Monogram 540 Mercedes. Door handles came from still another kit, as well as the rear-view mirrors seen on the side-mounted wheels.

Another example of extra detailing can be discovered in the photo of another Lincoln model. This one is the Locke Bodied Touring Car. Here are wire wheels made by inserting all new spokes of wire into the wheel rims, replacing the too few of the original wheels. Much

140

Plastic models of Hispano-Suiza cars from Spain—an Alfonso Roadster and a Town Car. (*Kirt Miska*)

of this model was reworked, including the making of new top bows and top boot of cardboard and wire. The boot covering is canvas with thread used for the beading around the edges. Leather is used for upholstery in both Lincoln models. Step plates shown on the Cabriolet's running board can also be used separately on cycle-fendered sport car models. So can spare wheel straps made from narrow leather strips, similar to those on the Cabriolet's spares.

A Mercedes K built of cardboard and some spare plastic kit parts to a scale of ¾ inch to 1 foot. (*Kirt Miska*)

This Bugatti was reworked from an inexpensive plastic kit. The photo fails to do it justice. (*Kirt Miska*)

Trunks made of cardboard, or plastic ones taken from a kit, can be covered with leather or canvas and mounted as shown on the Chrysler Roadster. Spotlights on either side of the windshield of this model are extra equipment. These lights are not standard with the kit and were left over from something else.

Instead of putting on detail, it is sometimes best to remove a part or section of a model in order to copy a particular custom-built classic car. A good illustration of this is the Jo-Han Mercedes Roadster. In order to give the fenders a long, flowing look, the skirts were trimmed off before assembly. After painting, chrome strips were run along the fenders' edges, helping to accent the desired sweeping lines.

A Rolls-Royce from Monogram with leather and cloth upholstery and cream and black paint. (*Kirt Miska*)

A custom-built 1931 La Salle model with rear windshield and covers for the spare tires. (*Kirt Miska*)

A leather interior and canvas-covered boot top were also extras for this Mercedes model. Added was a polished aluminum exhaust stack made of tubing. It can be seen at the rear of the car, and replaces the original plastic exhaust.

Monogram's Rolls-Royce with the hood off to reveal the engine, and with the rumble seat open. (*Kirt Miska*)

A Chrysler Imperial Roadster re-worked from the model of a convertible. The paint scheme was taken from color pictures in the Chrysler sales catalogue. (*Kirt Miska*)

A Duesenberg made from a Monogram plastic kit. It's hard to tell the model from the real car in this picture. (*Kirt Miska*)

A Lincoln touring car for seven passengers. Wire spokes were inserted in the wheels by the modeler because the plastic spokes seemed too heavy. (*Kirt Miska*)

A black and gray, super-detailed model from the Hubley metal kit. (*Kirt Miska*)

The Model 540K Mercedes plastic kit by Monogram makes a sporty car.
(*Kirt Miska*)

This Holbrook Cabriolet with a Lincoln chassis was made to exact scale from
parts of various kits. (*Kirt Miska*)

A 1912 Cadillac made from an early Revell kit, and completely rebuilt by the author. (*Kirt Miska*)

To go a bit further, a look at the photo of the Cadillac V-16 Touring Car will give you a clear idea of the beauty of line that a small change, such as removing the fender wells of the front fenders, can bring about. Little else needed to be done to this Jo-Han model except to wax the blue plastic and add leather to the interior. With the spare wheel mounted at the rear as the earlier model had, the entire appearance of the model was changed.

Some model car kits do not need any work because of the particular body styling, so the only thing you can do is to add details to the engine. The Monogram Bugatti Type 35B is one of these models. Spark plug wires, throttle and spark control levers and the belt for driving the magneto were all that was required. The body shell was waxed before assembly to take away some of the "plastic-color" look, and the brake cabling was added.

Since engine detailing has been mentioned, it is necessary to point out that a model maker should not attempt this unless he knows what he is doing and has good, sharp pictures of the engine, from

147

A V-16 Cadillac Touring Car from a Jo-Han kit, completely re-worked. The spare wheel was placed in its original position at the rear instead of on the running board. (*Kirt Miska*)

both sides. Only in such cases as the large Monogram Jaguar XKE where all needed wires and visible extras are part of the kit itself, the modeler may not need photos or drawings of the real car.

Leather or fabric covering of the car seats is usually a necessity for any fine model. Since most plastic models do not have this material in the kits, you have to purchase it extra.

A magnificent model of the Mercedes 500K Roadster from the Jo-Han kit. The swooping fenders are customized. (*Kirt Miska*)

The plastic body of this Cord model from Monogram is waxed. The hood opens. (*Kirt Miska*)

The best leather to use for model seats is very thin stock. Sometimes you can obtain it thinner than the leather used for ladies' gloves. This will form to almost any shape or curve readily. It can be fitted over seats and on inside pieces before they go into a model. Use Elmer's glue to make it stick. Various grades of fabric can also be used in the same way to make the seats have the mohair look found in the old sedans. Heavy fabric with deep pile can be used for floor rugs. These are cut to fit after the seats and sides are in place. Elmer's glue should be used for the rugs, too.

This Hubley Duesenberg Phaeton comes from a superb metal kit. (*Kirt Miska*)

Because this model is a bit larger than most, it lends itself to fine detailing.
(*Kirt Miska*)

The Packard Victoria Coupé built just as its parts came from the kit by Hubley,
without re-working of any kind. (*Kirt Miska*)

The Hubley metal Packard with its engine exposed. Much extra detailing went into this model. (*Kirt Miska*)

A Chrysler Imperial model with red leather upholstery and waxed plastic body. (*Kirt Miska*)

Even metal models like this early Rolls-Royce can be super-detailed. (*Kirt Miska*)

Two English electric track models (Scalextrics), a Bentley on the left, an Alfa-Romeo on the right, are in process of being re-built and super-detailed by following photos of the real cars. (*Kirt Miska*)

This dashing little racing car was made of laundry shirt cardboard in a few hours. Only the wheels, tires and radiator came from a plastic kit. (*Kirt Miska*)

Also peculiar to vintage and classic cars were such things as a windshield for the protection of the rear passengers in the open cars. The Hubley model of the Sport Touring Duesenberg, made of metal and plastic, shows this clearly. The Hubley Duesenberg comes in two styles—the Touring and the Town Car. Both are rather large in size and require a good bit of very interesting work to assemble. They are perfectly wonderful models to super-detail.

The Touring Car pictured has a special brown and black paint job, copied from a real car, and a leather-covered trunk that did not come with the kit. Also added are engine details such as wires, levers and rods. The interior is covered in tan leather with brown fabric rugs on the floor. Door handles are non-standard, as is the boot on the folded top.

If you want to, after you have purchased one or the other of the Hubley Duesenbergs or one of the beautiful Packard kits that they also manufacture, you can remove the fender wells, using a jeweler's blade in your jig saw handle. Fill in the hole and mount the twin spare tires on the rear of the car, leaving off the trunk or replacing it with a folded trunk rack.

The author worked on this brass scale model of the 1914 Mercer for a year. Complete inside and out, the springs work, the wheels steer, the hand brakes move. The upholstery is real leather. Detail is exceptionally fine. (*Kirt Miska*)

An author-built, 1923 Stutz Bearcat made of brass. The hood is raised to show details of the engine. (*Kirt Miska*)

Brass, scratch-built model of a 1914 Issota-Franschini Touring Car that is complete in all external details. (*Kirt Miska*)

Of course, in order to mount the spares at the rear, you will have to have some sort of tire mount. This can be bent to shape from number 20 brass wire and soldered together. Then the mount can be fitted into holes drilled in the back of the chassis or platform and securely glued in place. Naturally, the model maker has to have some idea of what a rear tire wheel mount looks like. If he doesn't, he will have to search through old photos, ads or books until he comes up with the right one to copy.

Windshield wings, the little side-mounted pieces of glass that you find fixed to each side of the windshield of some older cars, open or closed, were not always standard. Most of the time the owner purchased them and then had them fastened on at his personal order. They did help keep the wind from blowing into the front seat and made driving more pleasant. They also gave the car a sportier look. These windshield wings can be made from small pieces of clear plastic, the thickness of playing cards. You can cut the plastic with sharp scissors to the shape you want and smooth off the edges with a flat, fine X-acto file. Then the wind wings are glued in place. Be careful never to get the glue on the plastic, for it will ruin all your

155

Solido of France makes this collector's item—a Panhard chauffeur-driven Town
Car built to 1 to 43 scale.

careful work. You will find illustrations of these windshield wings
in many ads, shown as extra equipment in the automobile companies' sales catalogs. The same clear plastic can also be used for
light lenses.

The older cars had spare tire covers of canvas or leather. These
are not hard to duplicate. If you use thin leather, wet it and it will
stretch over the spare tires and form itself. Any excess is trimmed off
and Elmer's glue is used to hold the covers in place. Fabric that will
represent canvas can be applied in the same manner. Spare-wheel
covers can be seen in this book on the LaSalle Touring Car and the
Panhard-Levassor models.

Some cars had tool boxes fixed to the running boards, but they
were not always in the same position. Both the Voisin and the
Bentley models have them. These model tool boxes can be made up
of thin wood or bent from sheet aluminum. The real tool boxes
were usually of wood and mahogany in color and had brass fittings.
The brass metal boxes were polished bright or painted black, or the
same color as the car's body.

Kitchen aluminum foil comes in very handy for such things as aluminum floorboards, like those found on the Stutz Bearcat and the Mercer Runabout. You can use the foil on running boards, radiator shells, bumpers and step plates, or any place where a bright aluminum metal finish is needed. Just make certain that the foil is free from creases, wrinkles and bends. Use Elmer's glue to mount it. Press the foil in place with even strokes of your fingers. When the glue is dry, remove any excess foil with a sharp blade in your X-acto knife.

It would be easy to mention many more details that could be added to make your models better, but you will discover them and materials to use as you progress in your model making. The items mentioned are meant to serve as a guide and to help you use your imagination when constructing models. Just as you can super-detail the old cars, you can customize the modern automobiles. Included in most of these modern car kits, as well as in many of the airplane and speedboat kits, are custom parts which you can add to the model you choose. Different kinds of motors, motor equipment, wheels, radiator shells, seats, body parts, decals of many designs, different size tires and custom-designed chassis parts will be found in the car kits.

A fabulous model of the Bugatti Type 35B built from a plastic kit by Monogram.

This is the Renwal version of the 1966 "Revival" Pierce-Arrow.

The Renwal "Revival" model kits include a proposed design for a 1966 Packard, too. These kits are easy to put together.

A choice of squadron markings, and of parts to make either the original airplane or its improved model, including guns, several different arrangements for rockets, bombs, and the like, are discovered in the aircraft kits. The speedboat kits offer a choice of motor power and motor placement as well as color schemes and decorative decals.

So much is offered in kit form that there is no need for a lengthy description. You can see that for yourself when you go to your model shop. The kit instructions will give you all the information you need.

Plastic "Revival" kit for a 1966 Duesenberg. Renwal also makes kits for a future
Jordan, Stutz and Bugatti.

This Jo-Han model is a true copy of the most advanced American car—the actual
Chrysler Turbo-Car.

The model Napoleonic Coach built by the Junior Award winner, Howard Jennings, in one of the Fisher Body Craftsman's Guild contests.

However, it must be said that no matter how much and how beautifully the kits are made, you can only build a model well if you have the experience and the imagination and the patience that are required of any fine workman.

A word or two about the construction of plastic kits may not be out of place here, for there are several things to remember when you build them.

First, always read the instructions and look over the plans carefully, just as you did when building the models in this book.

Have a piece of sandpaper or a knife handy to scrape off the plating on chromed parts where they are to be glued on to something else. They will not stick together if you do not. A thin, pointed stick or a length of piano wire 6″ long should be used for applying the plastic cement. Whenever you use plastic cement, apply only a little to each surface. If you use too much cement it will ruin the appearance of the parts and the model.

This model won $4,000 second place prize for Michael Pietruska, aged 12, of Stamford, Connecticut.

Fit the parts together before you cement them. File, cut or sandpaper any excess material away until each part fits the other exactly. Plastic parts are not too strong. You cannot force them together without having them break in two. The best kit model makers always assemble all of the parts before they attempt to use plastic cement.

Most of the kit models are assembled according to a set number of steps. This should be strictly adhered to. Each part is usually numbered. Constantly check these numbers with those in the instructions so that you know you have the correct part and know where it goes. Also check the parts list and parts with the plans before you begin any model. Sometimes a part is missing and it may be a vital unit without which the model cannot be successfully assembled. The kit manufacturer will send you another. Wait for it no matter how anxious you are to start work.

Some parts do not look like the thing they are supposed to represent. This is usually because the unit is composed of more than one piece. Check the pieces, assemble them "dry" and you will find that it comes out properly.

Always clean the plastic parts of burrs, casting, mold lines and other imperfections. Also file flat any surface that is supposed to be flat, according to the plans or instructions. You will find that many of the supposedly flat ends and some edges have a slope or roundness to them. This is called "draft" and is done so that the parts can be taken out of the molds easily. Usually these must be made flat to give the parts proper fit and appearance.

The model made by 15-year-old Dwight G. Conger of Detroit, Michigan, won first place and $5,000.

The mold marks can be filed off with a flat X-acto file or scraped off with an X-acto knife, or sandpapered down with fine sandpaper. Whichever is easiest to use in a particular case should be used. A strip of sandpaper, for instance, is better than a knife or file on a round part. A file will do its best work on a flat surface having mold marks. A knife or blade is usually best when you have to get into places that are either narrow or irregular.

Plastic parts that are *not* plated can be held together with cellophane tape until dry if these parts are not too small or easily broken. Small or easily broken parts can be held together with pins inserted into a smooth board. Place the pins on either side, or the ends of the part, in much the same way as you did with the balsa-wood flying-model parts. Be careful that you do not get plastic cement on the pins or you may break the part anyway when you try to remove the pin from it.

Finally, if you wish to make certain that parts like muffler pipes or drive shafts line up exactly, draw a pencil line on your work board and use this as a guide. Place the parts over the straight pencil line, drawn with a ruler, and use pins to hold them in position until they have dried together.

Chapter 13

A Golden Opportunity for Model Makers

An opportunity to put one's interest in making models to practical use—and even to lead to a career in designing America's future automobiles—is presented by the Fisher Body Craftsman's Guild which for many years has carried on a program rewarding the skills, ingenuity and workmanship of young modelers through prizes awarded in annual competitions. The following, from an official release of the Guild, tells the story of the competitions and awards, and gives the requirements for entering the program.

"The Fisher Body Craftsman's Guild boasts a proud tradition of design excellence and superb craftsmanship dating back to the inception of its model-building competition in 1930.

"In that year, Fisher Body's interest in the development of technical and manual skill in the nation's youth, and the blending of America's educational curriculum of manual arts with academic arts, led to the formation of the Craftsman's Guild.

"By instituting this type of youth program, it was hoped that the development of craftsmanship and creative ability would be fostered. The program met with the immediate approval of leading educators.

163

"It was decided that the Guild would be sponsored by industry and guided by educational administrators and officials. Advisory and Honorary boards were set up to assist in the educational development of the Guild's program. Each year these boards meet with Guild officials to outline the objectives and assist in the growth and improvement of the competition.

"Boys between the ages of 11 and 20 are eligible for membership in the Guild. Extra-curricular in nature, the competition is divided into a junior division, age 11 to 15, and a senior division, age 16 to 20.

"The basis for the competition was originally the building of a model Napoleonic Coach, which symbolized a tradition of excellence among the old craft guilds. History shows that the coaches built in Napoleonic times were among the finest products of human handicraft in the world.

"Building a Napoleonic coach required skilled fingers, a fine eye and hours of tedious finishing work. All parts of the coach were hand fashioned and boys spent hundreds of hours on body decorations, wheels, upholstery and trim.

"The first year of the Guild competition proved to be highly successful. More than 145,000 boys enrolled in the Guild in 1930, and soon the program was recognized throughout the country by countless more American youths.

"More than 600 finished coaches were received the first year. The participants were awarded $50,000 in university scholarships and cash awards.

"To highlight the awarding of the scholarships, it was decided to bring the regional winners to Detroit for an awards banquet. The country was divided into 20 regions with a junior and senior winner from each receiving a four-day expense-free trip to Detroit. After the awards banquet, which was attended by national leaders of business, industry and education, the boys spent time visiting G.M. Styling, the proving grounds and other industrial facilities in the Detroit area.

"To supplement the instructions sent to each Guild member, the GUILDSMAN magazine was produced. Four issues were mailed to participants during the year with helpful suggestions about model building and stories about the success of fellow guildsmen.

"As the result of growing interest in the automobile in the mid-thirties, model cars of the boy's own design were allowed in the competition.

"After World War II, the Guild renewed its program and in 1948, the coach was retired from competition in favor of the model car.

164

"Nearly 600,000 Guild members are now enrolled in the annual competition. As models are received at Guild headquarters, they are unpacked, tagged and sent to the judging room. Professional stylists and industrial arts instructors evaluate the hundreds of models and select the winners.

"Fisher Body will present 1078 awards worth $117,000 to participants this year. Winners are selected at the state, regional and national level in each age group. The state awards are: 1st state—$150; 2nd state—$100; 3rd state—$50; and five honorable mentions of $25 each.

"The 50 states and the District of Columbia are divided into 20 population regions for judging purposes. For example, New York state is a region in itself, while Nebraska, Kansas, Oklahoma and Arkansas make up another region. The regional winners are invited to attend the four-day expense-free trip to Detroit where the national awards are announced at a special banquet.

"At the national awards banquet, eight major scholarships are awarded, four in each division. They are: 1st place—$5,000 scholarship; 2nd—$4,000 scholarship; 3rd—$3,000 scholarship; and 4th—$2,000 scholarship. In addition, ten $1,000 styling scholarships are awarded for design excellence regardless of division or region.

"To date, more than 8.7 million boys have enrolled in the competition and have been awarded in excess of $2.4 million in university scholarships and cash awards."

If you as a model maker are interested in participating in the Fisher Body Craftsman's Guild, write for information to the Guild at Warren, Michigan.

Herbert Lozier

has written more than 100 articles over the last 30 years on making models of aircraft, ships, automobiles, locomotives and the like. "One of the greatest thrills of my life," he recalls, "was the ten dollars that I received for an article on the construction of a fighter airplane made of cardboard. It was in 1939." Since then, Mr. Lozier's creative interests have led him through a wide range of endeavors including making models for the Museum of Science and Industry in New York, and work with Raymond Loewy, the industrial designer, for whom he made futuristic models of planes, cars, boats and trains. He became interested in antique and classic cars, and, as is the habit of the born collector, soon found himself neck-deep in the pleasure of fussing around with Cords, Auburns, Rolls-Royces, Lancias, Packards and others. He misses no longer having them, "but time and moving (from one place to another) played havoc with the collection."

Lozier's interest in old cars and in models and model making has resulted in the preparation of this book, and in one on the famous Mercedes cars, called *The Car of Kings*. He was born in 1915, and lives on Long Island, New York, with a string of pet cats. "They follow me out to the mailbox and back again every day," he says, "to the wonderment of the neighbors."